Editor
Stephanie Buehler, M.P.W., M.A.

Editorial Project Manager
Karen J. Goldfluss, M.S. Ed.

Editor-in-Chief
Sharon Coan, M.S. Ed.

Illustrator
Barb Lorseyedi

Cover Artist
Elayne Roberts

Art Director
Elayne Roberts

Imaging
David Bennett
Ralph Olmedo, Jr.

Product Manager
Phil Garcia

Publishers
Rachelle Cracchiolo, M.S. Ed.
Mary Dupuy Smith, M.S. Ed.

BUSY TEACHER'S SURVIVAL GUIDE

Timesavers, Techniques, and Tips from A to Z

Author

Barbara Danforth Martin

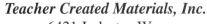

Teacher Created Materials, Inc.
6421 Industry Way
Westminster, CA 92683
www.teachercreated.com

©1996 Teacher Created Materials, Inc.
Reprinted, 2001
Made in U.S.A.
ISBN-1-55734-029-3

Teacher Created Materials

Table of Contents

*(**Note:** Italics indicate reproducible forms.)*

Table of Contents *(cont.)*

Table of Contents *(cont.)*

Table of Contents *(cont.)*

Table of Contents *(cont.)*

Introduction

Everyone knows that teaching is hard work, but it is one of the few jobs where one can come into contact with children on a daily basis and have a real impact on their young lives. With the waves of social change, teachers have become more than bearers of knowledge. They also function as counselors, social workers, authors of new curriculum, and experimenters in methodology. In short, teachers have responsibilities far beyond the scope of what we could have imagined only two decades ago.

This book is designed to help you with the nuts and bolts of classroom management so that you can focus your energy on the most important component of your teaching time—the students. When you are organized and have a handle on how to manage lesson plans, paper work, discipline, and so forth, you will find that you have more time to work on your students' skills.

On the lighter side, *The Busy Teacher's Survival Guide* is filled with ideas for subject areas that many teachers find challenging, such as art and physical education. The ideas are organized alphabetically so that they are easy to find when you are pressed for time.

Armed with ideas that work, you will be prepared for any situation—and that's what this book is all about. *The Busy Teacher's Survival Guide* has tips gleaned from years of experience—everything from starting the year off right to ways to fill those unexpected blocks of time. Whether you are a substitute teacher, new to the classroom, or have several years of teaching, this guide will be a helpful addition to your professional library.

A

Art

Introduction

You will find many well-proven art ideas in this section, but you should always be on the lookout for ideas from other teachers, instructors' and children's periodicals, and books purchased from the educational supply store. Art is a wonderful way for children to express themselves. Allow children ample time to experiment with materials and techniques; not every art period needs to culminate with a take-home project.

Grading Art

For many teachers, art is a difficult subject to grade. It may help to determine the purpose of the lesson first. For example, you would grade differently if the purpose were self-expression than if it were to follow directions for a project going up on bulletin boards in the school hallway. Let the students know the purpose before they begin.

Making Patterns

Make patterns twice as fast! When you need to make several tagboard patterns for students to trace, try stapling your original to two separate sheets of tagboard and then cutting them both out. Also, label both sides of the pattern pieces with the word "pattern" in large permanent marker; otherwise, students may take your pattern and decorate it instead of making their own.

Using Scissors

Tell students that when cutting, the paper should move, not the scissors. This will take a little getting used to if the children have not used scissors in this way before, but eventually they will be able to cut much more neatly.

To cut circles within a sheet of paper with blunt scissors, bend the paper just a little where the circle is to be and cut through the crease. From this opening cut spokes like a bicycle wheel. Now the curves between the spokes will be easy to cut as the paper is free to bend.

Using Watercolors

Teach children before they begin to paint that each color must be softened with water; to go from light colors to dark ones; and to mix colors on a palette. (Sheets of wax paper stapled to cardboard backs make a satisfactory palette.) Be sure to tell them to treat the brushes gently by swirling them, rather than jamming them, into cups of water to rinse.

When introducing watercolors, allow the students to spend several art periods just getting acquainted with the paint and brush, mixing new colors, and making colors lighter or darker by adding white or black. As part of their play, ask them to match their paints with three colors they find in the classroom and then to check each other's work.

Collect the paints by having the children bring you or the art monitor their open paint boxes to introduce the idea that they need to keep the paints clean and rinse out their brushes.

A

Art *(cont.)*

Month-by-Month Project Ideas

September

Fall Leaf Mobile: Start off the traditional year by having students paint fall-colored poster paint on red, orange, or yellow construction paper. After painting both sides of the sheet and allowing the paint to dry, have them cut out a variety of leaf shapes, including one large leaf, either from self-made or store-bought patterns. After the children cut out the leaves, they can make a mobile out of them with the small leaves hung with string of different lengths from the outside edge of the largest leaf. After the small ones have been hung, the students can find the center of balance for the large leaves by balancing the large leaves on the erasers of their pencils. Have them poke a hole there and push the string through. The mobiles are ready to hang from the classroom ceiling for a bright, happy look.

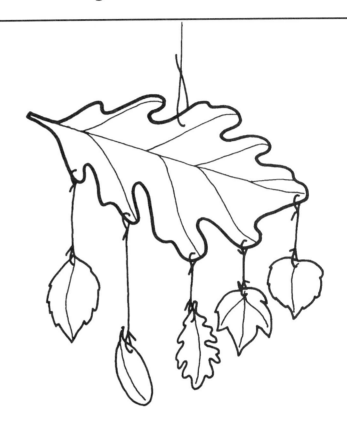

October

Jack-o'-Lanterns: Make construction paper yellow and orange jack-o'-lanterns to paste onto a black background. Younger children can cut out yellow paper features to glue onto the jack-o'-lantern; older students can cut the features out before pasting the pumpkin to the black background.

Ghost Pictures: Have students create irregular patches of color with heavy crayon on white drawing paper. After filling in the entire sheet, the whole paper needs to be heavily colored with black crayon. Students then use a partially unbent paper clip to scratch a picture on the black crayon. Boo! Colors appear! Be warned, though, that this project takes about two hours, so you may want to plan two sessions for it. It is also rather messy, so do not do it on a day you will have visitors!

Ghoulicious Cookies: Follow the directions on page 12. Some ideas to get them started are: "Lady Fingerettes" or "Goreos."

November

Thanksgiving Turkeys: Students reflect upon those things for which they are thankful as they create the Thanksgiving turkeys on page 13.

Butcher Paper Scenes: Have students draw a scene with an Indian-Pilgrim motif.

Art (cont.)

Month-by-Month Project Ideas (cont.)

December

Christmas Hands: Have students trace their hands many times onto dark and bright green construction paper. Then direct them to cut out their tracings and curl the paper fingers on the edge of the desk. (If a paper finger tears, just staple or tape it back on and use this tracing at the back of the project.)

Use the hands to
Decorate a three-foot tree on your bulletin board. You can add real satin balls and construction paper gifts along the bottom.

Cover wreath-shaped tagboard. Attach the wreaths to the classroom door with a sign saying, "Happy Holidays from Room __."

Form tagboard cones 12" (30 cm) in diameter and cover them with the students' hand tracings to make individual trees. Large sequins can be added to the tree. Paste gold stars on either side of the top—with most of the stars sticking to each other. Each student will have his or her own tree.

Christmas Gift Calendar: Children can make gift calendars for their parents. This takes a lot of time, so have the children create the calendar art one month per day for two to three weeks. Stationery stores will sometimes give you free calendars, or create your own master with regular and school holidays included and run it off. Children may also add days that are special to their families. Then create a picture for each month. Finish the calendar by punching a hole for hanging. Students who finish early can create covers and add their names as the artists.

Holiday Trees: Decorate a tree shape with sequins and glitter, or make a "lit" holiday scene with sequin-decorated houses.Or, make stained glass Christmas trees to decorate windows. (See directions on page 14.)

January

Snowflakes: See the snowflake pattern on page 15. Students enjoy making these and they are a good free time activity. You could also try dipping the edges of coffee filters in watercolors or food coloring and cut snowflakes from them when they dry. These beauties can be sprinkled lightly with glitter and hung from the ceiling. White paper snowflakes can be affixed to a blue bulletin board with the caption, "Every One Different, Every One Special."

Winter Scenes: Create a winter scene with snowmen or make a snow scene, using dark blue paper with thick white poster paint for snow. Add small, store-bought plastic snowflakes, clear glitter, or white construction paper snowflakes.

A

Art *(cont.)*

Month-by-Month Project Ideas *(cont.)*

February

Valentine's Day Card Holders: Have students make card holders using the pattern and directions on pages 16-17.

Heart Art: Show students how to make hearts from a sheet of paper folded in half by cutting out an ice cream cone. When unfolded, the students should have a good heart shape. Have them make large and small red and pink hearts to scatter around a Valentine's Day message.

March

Shamrocks: Make shamrocks from large and small tagboard patterns (See "Making Patterns" on page 8.) and let students use the shape to create a design such as a butterfly.

April

Spring Flowers: For Easter, make spring flowers from construction paper with edges curled and lambs from cotton. For students who do not celebrate Easter, a bouquet of construction paper tulips is an appropriate symbol of spring renewal.

May

Mother's Day Plates: Try making dishwasher safe plates for mother or a special female friend or relative. You can get instructions for having the plates made from Small Fry Originals Plastics Manufacturing Company, P.O. Box 769045, Dallas, Texas 75376-9045. The plates do cost money to have made—money most school districts do not have. One option is to hold some kind of fundraiser early in the year. Another is to simply have the students bring money from home, with discreet provisions for those students who do not have funds. A third idea is to collect aluminum cans from the first day of class and use the cash from recycling to purchase the plates.

Standing Picture Frames: These frames make wonderful Mother's Day gifts. Follow the directions on page 18.

Mother's Day Pictures: Create a special picture for mother (or a special female) for Mother's Day.

June

Father's Day Pictures: Create a special picture for father (or a special male) for Father's Day. Students can also make Father's Day cards using the directions on page 18.

July

Vacation Scenes or Fireworks: Have students draw a scene from their last vacation (or the vacation they wish they had had!) or use dark blue construction paper and white poster paint to create fireworks. Sprinkle glitter onto the paint while it is still wet or onto white glue painted on with cotton swabs. Do not use glue sticks for glitter; it comes off when the glue has dried.

August

Summer Scenes: Paint a desert or water scene.

Art *(cont.)*

Ghoulicious Cookies

Directions: You will be creating a special box advertising the Ghoul Scout cookies inside. You will need to bring a cookie or cracker box from home, or you can create one by enlarging and cutting the pattern below from tagboard.

Plan your drawings and advertising so that each panel of the box looks balanced. Use lots of adjectives to tell about the cookies you would like to sell. What do the cookies look like, smell like, taste like, or feel like in your mouth? Be sure to check spelling and then ask your teacher to proofread your work.

Next, plan an oral advertisement for your Ghoulicious cookies.

Give a good description that will sell your product. Why should people want to buy it? Tell them what your cookies will do for them.

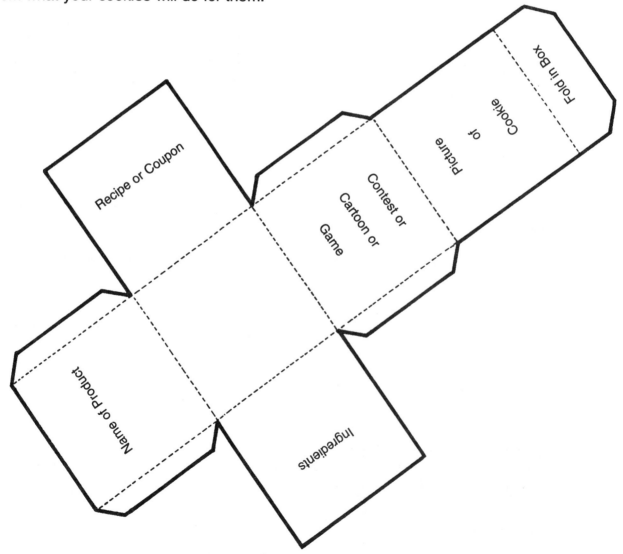

Art *(cont.)*

Thanksgiving Turkey

Before you begin your turkeys, work with the class to list things for which you are thankful on the board. Then get your supplies as follows:

Materials:

- sheets of 6" x 9" (15 cm x 23 cm) scrap paper
- one 6" x 9" (15 cm x 23 cm) sheet of dark brown construction paper
- one 6" x 9" (15 cm x 23 cm) sheet of light brown construction paper
- ten 1½" x 9" (3.8 cm x 23 cm) strips of construction paper in multi-colors
- one 2" x 4" (5 cm x 10 cm) piece of red construction paper
- scissors
- glue
- fine black marker or pencil

Directions:

1. Use scrap paper to practice making a half circle or hemisphere. When you are satisfied with the shape, trace it onto your dark brown construction paper. Add scalloped edges, if you like.

2. Cut a similar, but slightly smaller, hemisphere of the light brown construction paper. Glue it over the dark brown paper. Work neatly so that no glue or stray pencil marks will show in your finished work.

3. Fold the multicolored construction paper strips in half and cut in two. Use your scissors to shape one end of the strip to look like a feather.

4. On each paper feather, write one thing for which you are thankful. If you do not see your idea listed on the board, then you may ask the teacher for help with spelling.

5. Glue your feathers around the back edge of your turkey. Be sure your writing shows on the front.

6. Create the turkey's head and neck from a scrap of dark brown paper and then cut the wattle and feet from red construction paper. Glue these items onto your turkey. Add dark brown wings if you have time.

7. Use your fine marker or pencil to add details to your turkey.

Stained Glass Christmas Tree

These colorful ornaments make very attractive holiday window decorations.

Materials: tree pattern, oaktag, different-colored tissue paper cut in pieces approximately 3" x 4" (8 cm x 10 cm), glue, green construction paper, scissors

Directions: Trace the pattern below on tagboard. Cut out the pattern to use as a stencil. Trace around the oaktag stencil on green tissue paper. Cut out the tissue paper pattern on the back of the tree. Hang your tree up in a window and let the light shine through.

Art *(cont.)*

Snowflakes

Directions: Follow the diagrams shown below to create lacy snowflakes that are great for hanging in a window. Use a plain sheet of 8½" x 11" (22 cm x 28 cm) paper.

1. Fold the bottom right point so that the bottom edge meets the left edge of the paper. Cut off the rectangle remaining at the top of the sheet.

   Cut off.

2. Fold the bottom left point to meet the top right point.

3. In the same manner, fold the top left point to meet the top right point.

4. Fold the top left point to the right edge so that the left edge meets the right edge.

5. Cut off the triangle at the top.

   Cut off.

6. This shape will become your snowflake. Draw your pattern onto it so that on each side there will be paper left uncut; otherwise, you will have confetti! See the sample snowflake to get the idea, but please draw your own!

7. Try making snowflakes with straight lines only and with curved lines only. Choose and display your best example of each.

A

Art *(cont.)*

Valentine's Day Card Holder

Use the materials and directions below to make your own card holder.

Materials:

- patterns (page 17)
- scissors
- yarn
- masking tape
- single-hole punch
- pink and/or red paper
- markers or crayons
- candy hearts (optional)

Sample of Finished Project

Directions:

1. Cut out the bottom and top hearts on page 17.

2. Punch holes at the dots in both hearts.

3. Cut a length of yarn (about 2 feet/.6 meters). Wrap a piece of masking tape tightly around one end so that you can sew with it.

4. Place the top heart over the bottom heart. Make sure to line up the holes.

5. Starting at the top center hole of the top heart (marked with an X), sew together the two hearts, leaving enough of an end so that you can tie a bow when you are finished. (You will notice that the top heart has holes at the top, while the bottom heart does not. This is designed to leave an opening at the top of the card holder.) Continue threading the yarn through the holes. Finish at the top by tying a bow. (See the illustration above.)

6. Decorate the front of your card holder with markers or crayons or glue on small candy or paper hearts.

7. Staple the card holder to a bulletin board or other area of the classroom, as directed by your teacher.

8. Bring Valentine's Day cards to put in your classmates' holders.

Art *(cont.)*

Valentine's Day Card Holder *(cont.)*

Teacher's Directions: Enlarge these patterns 200% and reproduce them on construction or index paper. Use red or pink paper. Distribute the patterns to students and have them follow the directions on page 16. (An alternative to using these patterns is to cut out large and small heart patterns from tagboard or other heavy paper and have students use each pattern as a stencil. They can then punch out holes around each heart and follow steps 3–8 on page 16.)

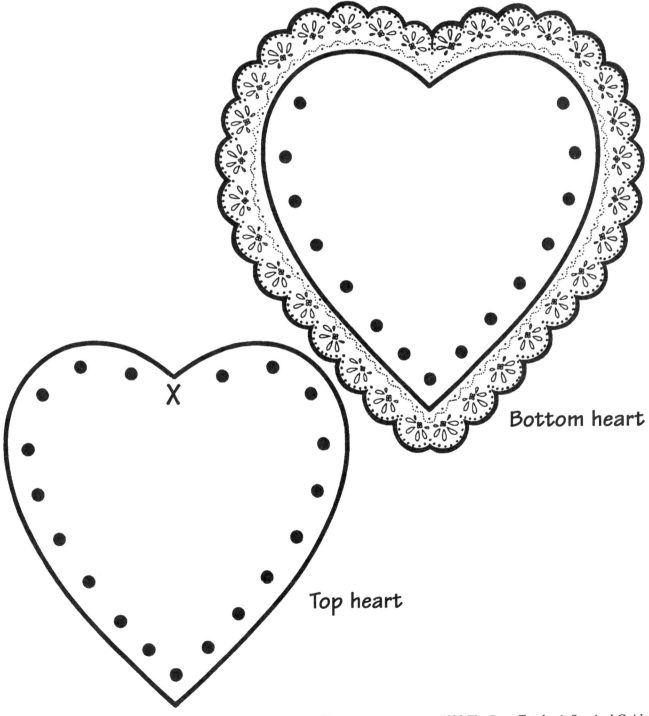

Bottom heart

Top heart

Art *(cont.)*

Standing Picture Frame

Have students follow the directions below to create their own very special picture frames. You will need construction paper (spring colors), glue, scissors, and crayons for this activity.

Directions: Enlarge and reproduce the patterns below on construction paper. Color the design on the frame front. Cut out all the pieces. Fold the frame front in half. Cut along the solid lines to cut out the center rectangle. Unfold the frame front. Glue the front frame to the back frame along the two sides and the bottom. To make the stand, fold flap F to the right and flap E to the left. Glue C and D together. Glue E and F to the frame back, making the bottom edge even with the bottom edge of the frame. Slip a picture between the front and back frames so it shows through the rectangle.

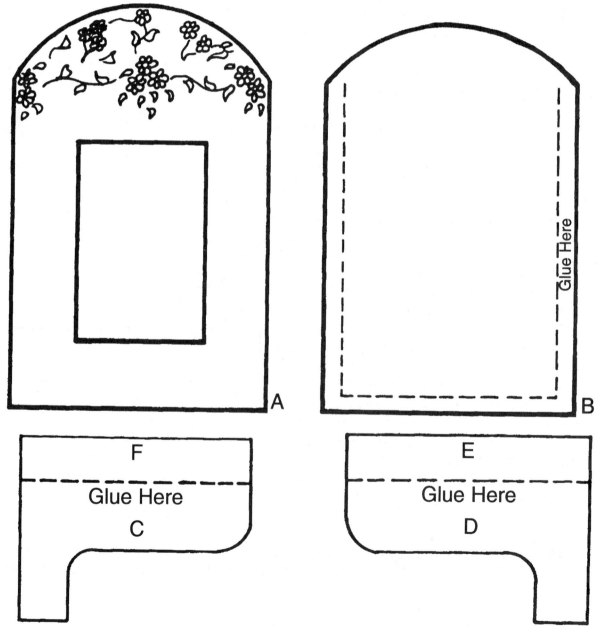

Attending Conferences

Try to attend a conference every year. We all need to get new ideas and to be inspired and recharged. Some groups and presenters are better than others, so if you see a brochure that interests you, ask other teachers for their recommendations. It may be possible to get your school or district to pay the conference fee, so be sure to check. But even if you must pay for the conference out of your own pocket, you may get enough ideas to get you through an entire year and beyond.

Awards, Rewards, and Raffle Tickets

Students need recognition for their efforts in learning. Many students do not receive recognition at home, and awards and raffle tickets help keep students motivated.

Awards: Give them for doing well on speeches, tests, memorizing poems, etc. Have awards to go along with each season, holiday, and even subject areas. You can purchase awards at an educational supply store or make a generic one on the computer, changing the graphic with the season. If you want the awards to look more handwritten, keep blanks in your drawer, pull one out as needed, and fill in the date and what the award is for, and sign your name. Then after running it off on the copier (try using colored copier paper), use the same pen to fill in the students' names. It will look as if each child has had one made just for him or her.

Raffle Tickets: Raffle tickets are easy to use and take little class time to prepare and distribute. (Some teachers prefer to buy raffle tickets. They are sold in large rolls and can be purchased at office supply stores.) Staple raffle tickets to good papers when you return them. Hand tickets to students who return forms the first day or for good sportsmanship. Give tickets to the whole class if they are working quietly in the library, etc. Then have a drawing on Friday for special pencils, food treats, books you've obtained with bonus points from the book clubs, posters, etc. Be crafty and ask for goodies at card shops, office supply stores, etc.

Rewards: Candy is cheap, so you may want to keep a tightly covered container in your class for quick rewards. If you feel you should not give students sugar, then tiny boxes of raisins or a handful of peanuts might make a better reward.

Back to School

Back-to-School Night can be intimidating, even for experienced teachers, so if you feel nervous, just remember—you are not alone!

Try convincing your students with the promise of a homework pass (see page 53) to bring their parents to your room first so that you can have a group gathered together; then, you will not have to repeat yourself over and over as newcomers appear.

Before Back to School begins, write your schedule on the board to go over with parents. Review your homework policy and give the hours at school when you are available to encourage two-way communication. Then open up the session for questions. Discourage individual conferences; if a parent is truly concerned, make an appointment to discuss the child's progress.

Have a sign-up sheet for parent volunteers next to the sign-in sheet. A sample sign-up sheet is provided on page 21.

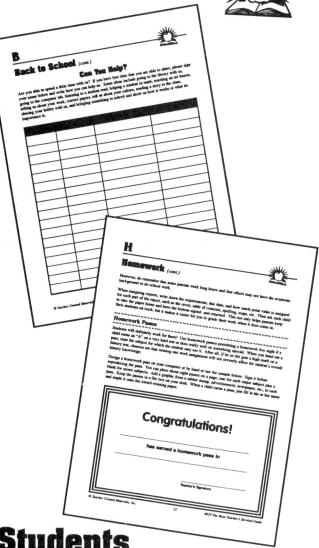

Bathroom Breaks for Students

This can be a problem area. You certainly do not want to have accidents in your classroom, but you also do not want children coming and going while you are teaching, either. The best policy is to make sure students use the restroom at recess and lunch unless it is an emergency. For younger children, be sure to clarify what constitutes an emergency. Most children will catch on quickly; those who do not can be dealt with on an individual basis, perhaps by allowing them a single bathroom pass after lunch or as needed.

Caution: There may be a medical reason the child needs to use the bathroom frequently. Refer the child to the school nurse and discuss the problem with the child's parents. Of course, if there is a medical need, the child should be allowed to use the bathroom as often as necessary.

Bathroom Breaks for You

Protect your health and take a bathroom break as needed. One of the biggest medical dangers to teachers is bladder infections—for men as well as women. Find out what the procedure is for bathroom breaks because this can differ from school to school and district to district. Do not forget to find out how to get a break when there is inclement weather and the children are eating lunch in the classroom.

Back to School *(cont.)*

Can You Help?

Are you able to spend a little time with us? If you have free time that you are able to share, please sign your name below and write how you can help us. Some ideas include going to the library with us, going to the computer lab, listening to a student read, helping a student in math, teaching an art lesson, telling us about your work, correcting papers, telling us about your culture, reading a story to the class, sharing your hobby with us, and bringing something to school and showing us how it works or what its importance is.

Your name	Student's name	What you can do to help	When

Thank you!

Book Reports

Book reports may sound old fashioned to students, but if you think "multimedia," they need not elicit groans from your students. You can require them weekly or monthly. Use the following list to give students plenty of ideas.

Book Report Ideas

Here are ten great ideas for book reports.

1. Create a new cover for your book. Include a summary about the book and author information on the flaps.

2. Write an ad for your book. Persuade other students to read your book.

3. Make a movie of your book. Put it on a paper scroll and attach each end of the scroll to a cardboard tube. Find a box and cut a viewing hole in the front and holes on the sides to hold the tubes. Students can watch the "movie" by turning the paper tubes.

4. Create a diorama of your book. Turn a shoe box on its side. Paint a background to fit a scene in your book and add characters made of paper or clay. Write a description of the scene inside the diorama.

5. Write a song about your book. Tell the story of the main character in ballad form.

6. For nonfiction, extend your knowledge. Read a second book on the same subject. Then compare the books, telling what is the same about them and contrast the books, telling what is different.

7. Create a game about your book. Make a game board that includes important settings, such as "100-Acre Woods" or "The Rabbit Hole." On some squares, indicate that the player is to draw a card. Create a card deck that has information related to the book. Be sure to have a great ending for your game.

8. Write a new story about the main character in your book. What new adventure would be great to send him or her on? Illustrate your story.

9. Create a pop-up type poster for your book. Draw an appropriate setting with windows and doors (or other appropriate ideas). Cut the windows and doors three-quarters of the way open. Glue this onto a sheet of blank paper. Then lift the windows and doors and write in facts about the characters.

10. For nonfiction, if possible, take a related field trip on your own time with an adult from home. Write a report about your trip, relating what you learned to the book that you read.

Bulletin Boards

Research shows that children notice a new bulletin board for only about a week; after that it loses its novelty, and the children no longer notice it at all. This doesn't mean that bulletin boards aren't worth the effort, as they can be good teaching tools. Students like to see their own work in class and frequently enjoy reading others' papers. But for one or two bulletin boards, it is perfectly all right to make or buy posters that you can leave up all year. Use borders that tie in with subjects, such as history or math instead of seasons so that all you have to do is change the students' work.

Some teachers have a "Star of the Week" bulletin board, displaying each student's picture in turn. The star student can bring items from home to put up on his or her board. Also, other students write words or phrases about the week's star.

You can also try a bulletin board with pictures, posters, or cartoons without their captions. Add a blank piece of paper and have the students add their own captions. They can then vote on the best caption at the end of each week.

Setting up Bulletin Boards

Letters: If you want a level line, the easiest way to put up letters is to measure down at the right side of your board and again at the left. Put in pins and stretch a string between. This will make your letters straight enough for the toughest critic! If you want your letters to be centered, find the middle of both the board and of the caption and work your way out to the ends.

Borders: Measure the circumference of each board once and keep a tagboard template so you do not have to measure each time you make a border. See "Posters" and "Starting Off the Year" for more ideas on borders.

Buying from Catalogs

Use catalogs to order many things, whether or not your school has a budget for each teacher. Use sticky notes to mark pages where there are items you would like to buy or keep a wish list, which is especially helpful when money suddenly becomes available. The teachers' magazines like *Learning* or *Instructor* have advertisements, postcards to send for free catalogs, and resource pages in the back to get catalogs. Get on at least one mailing list, and you're sure to receive many! See page 97 for a variety of resource materials.

Chalkboard Lines

Lines on the chalkboard are good for you and great for the students. Use a green permanent marker and a 2" (5 cm) board. Either mark both sides of the chalkboard every two inches using a ruler to use as guidelines for the board, or have two helpers hold and move the 2" board while you draw the lines. The lines wear off after awhile, so plan to redraw them when this occurs.

Choosing Student Monitors

Using regular monitors helps prevent the need to constantly choose helpers. When there is an un-monitored job and you want to choose someone impartially, toss a die. The first roll decides which table or row is to be chosen to go first and the second roll decides which student in that row or table will be selected if you only need one child to do a job.

Classroom Calendars

Especially if you are teaching primary grades, have a large calendar in the room. Buy large blank calendars at the educational supply store and laminate them. White and orange are good colors for year-round use. You can also buy all kinds of seasonal cutouts with dates on them; punch a hole in each one so you can hang it on a pin on the calendar. Have a student add the date each day. Hang numbers right beside the calendar in a stack or sprinkle them around the calendar, which can lead to a helpful lesson in number recognition.

If you are teaching primary grades, talk about the day of the week, which day of the week comes next, any special things that will be happening on that day, etc. In the upper grades, the calendar is not as important, but you can use the calendar bulletin board to display students' holiday art. If you change the number cutouts and the name of the month, this display is everchanging, with very little effort on your part.

Classroom Pets

Many children do not have pets at home, so, if you can bear to have one—or more—please do. An aquarium is very little trouble, and everyone likes to watch the fish. Or you might try to get some more interesting pets, like African frogs. Students can enjoy watching the African frogs shoot up to the top, take a breath, and go back down. However, you might not want an aquarium if you do not have a sink in your room. Of course, the more traditional pets, such as guinea pigs, gerbils, and turtles are a welcome addition to the classroom too!

24

Classroom Pets *(cont.)*

Rats make great pets. They are very smart, and they do not bite as cuter hamsters tend to do. A snake—especially a rosy boa—is another great classroom pet. Many kids have never touched a snake or even seen one up close, and these small, slow-moving, sociable animals are wonderful. You do have to feed a boa a mouse about once a month, but that means that you only have to clean the cage once a month, too.

Allow students to take home class pets over all breaks except summer; for that period you will want to take responsibility. Tell them that they must have a signed note from their parents and that the first student who brings a note gets the animal. The form on page 26 allows you to spell out specifically what both the classroom monitor and the vacation caretaker must do to ensure the pet stays alive.

Cockroaches and Ants

Here's a recipe from a custodian that really does the trick to get rid of these pests: Mix half powdered boric acid with half powdered sugar and sprinkle it in corners, behind files and bookcases, etc. This method is cheap and efficient!

Ants can sometimes come in and eat the weirdest things, like the plants you're growing for science. If you have a problem, check the nearest Asian grocery store if it sells something called ant chalk. You can put it around your pet cages, plants, etc. It will be a very long time before ants cross the chalk line.

Correcting Papers

You will save a lot of time correcting papers if you make sure children understand the directions and then allow them to work awhile in class to make sure the work is understood. Any work not completed in class can automatically become homework.

Studies show that the faster the feedback, the more effective it is, so have students correct their own papers. Students can also switch papers and correct each other's work and then switch back to see how they did.

At this point, it makes sense to collect the students' papers and correct them before recording grades. But if you do not have time to correct every problem, it is valid to spot check student papers. Then, if you see a real problem, you can circle the errors and return them to the student to be fixed, or if the student genuinely did not understand the assignment, offer assistance.

When you have finished recording the grades, put the papers in a box on your desk. All papers which need to be passed out go in there, unless it is urgent, in which case the paper monitor can return them right away.

Also try using transparencies for checking word searches or matching exercises. Make blanks and then fill them in as a template.

Classroom Pet Letter Form

"For Pet's Sake"

Dear _____ ,

To ensure that our classroom pet, _____, stays in tiptop shape, please follow these suggestions and reminders:

1. _____

2. _____

3. _____

4. _____

5. _____

6. _____

7. _____

8. _____

9. _____

10. _____

Thank you for making sure our classroom pet is well taken care of and happy.

Sincerely,

_____

WE HAVE
A
CLASSROOM
PET

C

Creative Writing

It's a good idea to tie creative writing topics with other subjects you are studying. But you will always need additional ideas; there are some very good resource books available for creative writing ideas. The *Write All About It* series (TCM 501–503) from Teacher Created Materials (Teacher Created Materials, Inc., 1993) provides excellent activities that help the students develop the writing process and strengthen their writing skills.

Start creative writing very simply by teaching the students how to write the title, an introductory sentence, three main sentences, and a closing sentence. Keep a long list of topics in your lesson plan book to remind you of how slowly you need to go in the beginning. Add extra ideas throughout the year.

Try to make a comment in pencil at the end of every student's paper—that way they can erase it if they want to. Do not correct everything and make them rewrite it—just ask them to work on one or two things the next time around.

Story Starters

1. I Like (Dislike) Dogs for Three Reasons
2. The Cafeteria
3. If I Were Principal
4. My Three Wishes
5. The Day It Rained Chocolate Pudding
6. If I Were a Witch
7. Three Things I Do Well
8. Mystery of the Missing Turkey
9. A Secret I Wish I Could Tell
10. The Past
11. Trips I Would Like to Take (two reasons for each trip)
12. Why Money Is Important
13. I Woke Up Before Sunrise
14. I Am a Shoe (with a drawing)
15. Unemployed Elf (a job application)
16. If Water Ran Uphill
17. Someone I Would Like to Work For
18. If Tomorrow Were My Last Day on Earth
19. An Odd Job
20. What I Can Do to Help the World
21. My Friend
22. My Year 2000
23. The Worst Day I Have Ever Had
24. If I Were 18
25. If I Were Invisible
26. Why Turtles Make the Best Pets
27. If I Ruled the World
28. If I Could Give (Receive) a Present
29. If I Could Be Someone Else
30. If It Always Rained on Saturday
31. If Animals Could Talk
32. If I Could Meet Anyone I Wanted To
33. If I Were a Parent
34. When I Get Mad at My Friend
35. What I Would Like to Do This Summer
36. If I Were the President
37. When I Have My Own Car
38. Next Year My Parents and I Will . . .
39. When My Brother (Sister) Got Me in Trouble
40. My First Job

D

Discipline

Classroom Rules

The key to a good set of classroom rules is to keep them simple. Have a class discussion to develop your rules. Be sure that the rules that are important to you and your teaching are included. The basic rules may be something like this:

Classroom Rules

☞ 1. Keep hands, feet, and objects to yourself.

☞ 2. Follow directions.

☞ 3. Do not talk unless called upon.

☞ 4. Stay in your seat unless given permission to get up.

☞ 5. Complete assignments.

Individual Discipline Plan

Some students have persistent behavior problems, and they will need to have some kind of an individual discipline plan written for them. With these students it is best to focus on only one thing to improve at a time. Consider what it is that bothers or interrupts you, the class, or the student the most, and write it down. Decide on the consequences for the behavior. The final consequence should be removal from the classroom. Do not forget to include a positive side to the discipline plan for the student. There needs to be some reason for him/her to want to follow the plan. Here is a format to use for writing an individual discipline plan.

Individual Discipline Plan

Student's Name:_____ **Date:** _____

Behavior to be improved: _____

_____

_____

Consequences: _____

Reward: _____

To get reward: _____

D

Discipline *(cont.)*

Time on Task

Time on task has to do with how much time students actually spend working on the lesson in class. When people visit your classroom, they see a variety of things, including how the students are engaged in the learning. If students are not attending to the lesson, the teacher needs to be aware of it because this is wasted time for both the student and the teacher. Time on task is related to how well you manage your students and lessons. Of course, students who have learning difficulties also have trouble with time on task because they seem to disengage themselves from the learning. Teachers need to notice and reinforce time on task behavior in order to maximize student learning.

Pointing Out the Positive

Teachers have two choices. They can point out all the negatives in the classroom or they can focus on the positive. It seems healthier to point out the positive. When teachers point out the positive behavior of individual students, it does two things.

First, it gives that individual student recognition and makes him want to continue that behavior. Secondly, when other students hear the comments, they usually want to get recognition and will also display the appropriate behavior. This works especially well in elementary school.

Some students, on the other hand, get into the habit of doing negative things to get attention. When the teacher "rewards" the negative behavior with the student's desired consequence—attention—the negative behavior may increase. As teachers, we need to be on the alert for this cycle, because if we get trapped into giving attention for negative behavior, we will be spending a lot of time and energy developing something negative.

Rewards

Rewards can be intrinsic or extrinsic. Intrinsic rewards are the kinds of rewards that come from within the individual. If you really enjoy working in the garden or cleaning house because you like the feel of getting "into the job" or doing the job itself feels good, it is intrinsically rewarding. Rewards that come from the outside, such as a compliment because the yard or house looks good, are extrinsic rewards. Neither kind of reward is more valuable; however, you can not always get extrinsic rewards when you want them. So, it is good to help students to develop a sense of pride in their good behavior so that it becomes intrinsically rewarding.

D

Discipline (cont.)

Reinforcement Theory

According to reinforcement theory, reinforcing or ignoring certain types of behavior will cause students to continue or eliminate specific behaviors. There are three kinds of reinforcement—positive, extinction, and negative. In positive reinforcement you reinforce those behaviors that are desired so that they will continue.

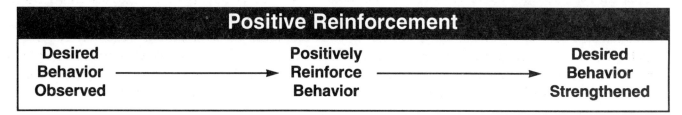

In extinction, you ignore undesirable behavior and positively reinforce desirable behavior in order to continue the desired behavior.

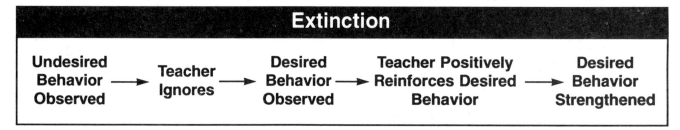

In negative reinforcement, you see the negative behavior and teach the student a replacement behavior. Also tied with this is a consequence. Now the student chooses the appropriate behavior or the consequence of choosing the undesirable behavior. This is different from punishment in that punishment comes after a behavior has occurred and the student has no choice.

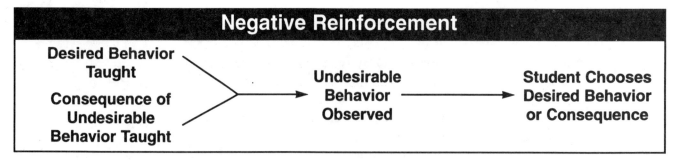

Scheduling is the frequency with which reinforcement occurs. One type of scheduling is regular reinforcement. In this type, each time the appropriate behavior is demonstrated, it is reinforced.

After students continue to demonstrate the desirable behavior, you may wish to move to the next kind of scheduling, which is intermittent reinforcement. Students may have become so used to the regular reinforcement that it no longer serves its purpose. Intermittent reinforcement assures that the behavior is continued while the students wait for (and occasionally receive) reinforcement. Students pay in, like a slot machine, and eventually reap the rewards.

D

Discipline *(cont.)*

Attention or Quiet Signals

What do you use to get the attention of your students when they are working? It is hard for the "teacher look" to work when they are happily working on a group activity or not looking at you and talking as they work. One of the best treats a teacher can do for herself is to teach the class one or two signals for when she wants the attention of her students. You may need several signals depending on what type of activity students are engaged in—what works for a quiet classroom probably will not work on the playground! The other key is that you need to TEACH the signal, just as you would a math problem or a vocabulary word. After you have taught the signal, the students will need to have time and opportunity to practice it. If their practice is great, tell them so. If it is not, tell them that they will need to practice the signal again until they can do it just right and MEAN IT. If you accept less than good attention, that is just what they will learn to give you. Reward students when they respond appropriately to the signal. You may need to practice occasionally if they slip.

When deciding on the signal for your class, consider the age, grade, ability level, and maturity of the group. Just because it worked with the same grade level last year does not mean that it will work well with this group. Here are some possible signals:

Raised Hand—Teacher raises his or her hand, and then the students stop talking, look at the teacher, and raise their hands until the class is ready.

Bell, Piano Chord, or Musical Tone—Students stop working and talking and put their heads down.

Clapped Rhythm—Teacher claps a rhythm, and the students clap either a responding rhythm clap or repeat what the teacher clapped and then look at the teacher.

Whistle Signal—Students freeze and look at the teacher.

D

Discipline *(cont.)*

Awards and Rewards

Rewards that you can use at school fall into three major categories—recognition, privileges, and tangible rewards. No single kind of reward works better than another. Select rewards for students depending on the grade level and preferences of the students. This is but a partial list of the kind of rewards you might decide to use. Be sure to add your own ideas as you think of them!

Privileges
- lunch with the teacher
- library pass
- computer use time
- pass for skipping homework
- peer tutor other students
- special art project
- special helper for the day
- choice of some activity
- work on a special project, game, center, etc.

Recognition
- telephone call to parents
- name in class or school newspaper
- hug, smile, or pat on the back
- display work
- class cheer, chant, etc.
- student of the day, week, month
- note sent home to parents
- announcement to the class
- recognition in daily announcements or at flag ceremony

Tangible Rewards
- stars
- popcorn party
- stickers
- paper bookmarks
- bonus points or extra credit
- educational video or movie
- snacks, treats in the classroom
- grab bag or treasure chest
- stamp for ink pad
- pencil, eraser, pencil top
- tokens for no homework, extra recess, etc.

D

Discipline (cont.)

How Do I Handle These Problems?

Disagreements Between Students: Whether students are having an argument or an actual fight, when they have calmed down enough to talk, ask each one in turn what happened. The other is to listen quietly without interrupting. The students keep taking turns until one story is agreed upon. If it is taking too long and they have still not agreed—and are calm enough—ask them to step outside the door where you can see them and finish their discussion there so that you can continue with the class. They can come back in when an agreement is reached. After they have agreed on one version, ask them each in turn where their own fault lay and what they should have done. If the situation is serious enough, ask them to write a letter to their parents (check it before it goes home), telling their parents what happened, what they did wrong, and what they plan to do next time.

Swearing: Have students write a letter to their parents, writing down exactly what they said and include that their teacher was not happy to have them say it at school and wanted their parents to know. It must come back signed by either one or both parents.

Talking, Individual Students: For those students who talk constantly, try this idea. Give the student three colored index cards. Every time the student talks during a period, hold out your hand for a card. When the student has no more cards to give you, the student is sent to another class until the beginning of the next period. If the student returns and talks again, back out they he or she goes. After the student has the ability to stay quiet for a period, extend the time to two periods, a morning, or even the day. Be sure to praise quiet times.

Talking, the Whole Class: Try some of the following methods to discourage excessive talking in the classroom: flick the lights on and off as a reminder that the talking must be stopped; have students raise their hands when they see yours raised (if they are working noisily in groups, this may take a while); clap your hands in a "shave-and-a-haircut" pattern, leaving the last two claps to them, etc. Some teachers try whispering; others stand quietly to model the behavior they want to see. Try them all until you find one you can live with and that works.

> We all function better when there are boundaries, and most children enjoy having a classroom where rules are understood and the consequences are clear.

Students also will enjoy class more if you are not wasting precious classroom time with discipline. You will also find that you have more energy to devote to teaching when you have a handle on managing the students' behavior.

File Folders

File folders can be used for a wide variety of projects and activities in the classroom—not to mention the filing purposes for which they were intended. Try to purchase or request file folders with five tabs because it is easier to see the tabs. You can buy gummed labels and use the folders on both sides until the tab has disintegrated, but file folders are relatively inexpensive, so you may just want to treat yourself to a fresh one as needed. You can recycle the old ones for students to use by clipping off the tab. Colored file folders can be helpful for current masters, weekly student report forms, spelling lists, etc. Colored folders just make things easier to find! Try them for things you frequently pull from your file drawers.

Consider buying metal holders for hanging files for your desk drawers that have vertical partitions. They are actually much easier to get things out of than the horizontal ones.

Flash Cards

Educational supply stores sell small, blank flash cards so you do not have to use larger, more expensive index cards for your students. Flash cards are not just used for reviewing math facts. Use them for memorizing states, countries, etc. Students can cut up their own photocopied maps and glue the states or countries on flash cards to study at home or with partners.

Use flash cards to play "Around the World." Have the first student in the first row stand behind the next student and flash a card at him or her. The first one to answer correctly gets to move to the next chair. When the person standing is incorrect, he or she sits down where he or she is. The first student to go "Around the World" by going around the class until returning to his or her own seat wins.

Free Time

Be clear about what students may or may not do once they have finished their work. One way to handle students who finish early is to allow them to circulate and help other students. Another is to allow them to correct activity sheets for you. A third idea is to let them keep their own list of approved free-time activities. The advantage with the latter is that it becomes a contract between you and the student. If a student is finished and is bothering others, have him or her refer to their contract for an approved activity. Have students fill out the form on page 35; then both of you should sign it.

My Free-Time Activities

I agree that when I have finished with my work, I will choose one of the following activities:

1. _____
2. _____
3. _____
4. _____
5. _____
6. _____
7. _____
8. _____
9. _____
10. _____

Student _____

Teacher _____

My Free-Time Activities

I agree that when I have finished with my work, I will choose one of the following activities:

1. _____

2. _____

3. _____

4. _____

5. _____

6. _____

7. _____

8. _____

9. _____

10. _____

Student _____

Teacher _____

G

Games

On page 37 is a list for outside and inside games. Keep the game checklist in your lesson plan book so that you can check off the games as you play them during the year. In addition, try to buy board games to keep in the classroom for rainy days or very smoggy ones when students are not allowed outside. In these days of video games, many students do not have any board games at home, or even a deck of cards! Time spent in class playing these games is not wasted. Children need to learn to take turns, to follow directions, to share, to learn the vocabulary, logic, and sportsmanship of these games—they differ from outdoor games and video games.

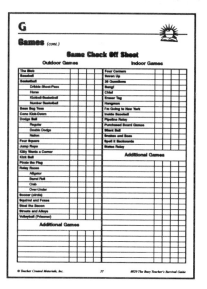

Board games help strengthen a variety of important skills. Keep a supply of board games in the classroom for a rainy day and free-time activities.

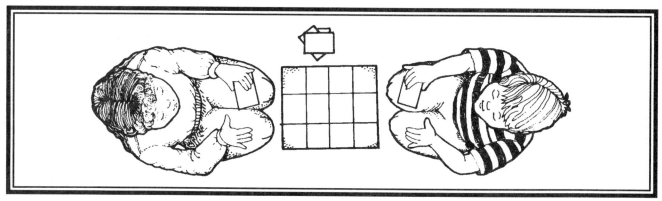

Picking Teams

Children love to be on the winning team or on a team with their friends, but it is a good idea to mix them up so that they can learn good sportsmanship. An easy way to do this is to line them up and have them count off numbers, sometimes up to four. Then mix up the way you put the numbers together to form the teams.

You can also let team captains pick teams, but after the choosing of the first six students or so, count off the remaining students. It is just too embarrassing for the ones who are not picked to be left until the bitter end.

Many schools have rules written down for games. Please check to see if they exist before you try to teach children games you grew up with. The rules and ways to play vary a great deal, and you may be teaching the students something which goes against the school's rules or something the children already have decided on their own. Be careful, or you may have a quiet rebellion on your hands.

Also, you might find out from them if there are any games they know from an old school, camp, etc., that they would like to play or would be willing to teach the class.

Games *(cont.)*

Games Check-Off Sheet

Outdoor Games					Indoor Games				
The Blob					Four Corners				
Baseball					Seven Up				
Basketball					20 Questions				
Dribble-Shoot-Pass					Bang!				
Horse					Chief				
Kickball-Basketball					Eraser Tag				
Number Basketball					Hangman				
Bean Bag Toss					I'm Going to New York				
Cone Kick-Down					Inside Baseball				
Dodge Ball					Pipeline Relay				
Regular Dodge Ball					Purchased Board Games				
Double Dodge Ball					Silent Ball				
Nation Dodge Ball					Snakes and Bees				
Four Square					Spell It Backwards				
Jump Rope					States Relay				
Kitty Wants a Corner					**Additional Games**				
Pirate the Flag									
Relay Races									
Alligator									
Barrel Roll									
Crab									
Over-Under									
Soccer (Circle)									
Squirrel and Foxes									
Steal the Bacon									
Streets and Alleys									
Volleyball (Prisoner)									
Additional Games									

Outdoor Games

The Blob

Equipment: A field with marked edges. Mark off a rectangular area about the size of three baseball diamonds with cones.

To play: One volunteer is selected. He or she is "The Blob." The student tags anyone he or she can find, and they, too, turn into Blobs and try to tag others. A player who becomes a Blob must always hold the hand of at least one other Blob. However, when the Blob gets up to four people, they may split into two pairs, making two separate Blobs. Play continues until only one player is not a Blob. When the player is caught, the game begins again. The last player to be tagged is the first Blob.

Baseball

Equipment: baseball and bat, diamonds, a backstop, and a tee, if possible

To play: Try using a tee or have a team pitch to itself. A batter gets three chances to hit—either pitched or on the tee—and then the hitter is out. Encourage students to try hitting two pitches and then switch to the tee.

Basketball

Dribble-Shoot-Pass

Equipment: basketball court and a basketball for each team—team size may vary

To play: You can play this like a relay, with the first team completing its cycle winning, with each team keeping count of its score on two or three cycles, or just as warmup practice.

Divide the class into as many teams as you have baskets, each team having its own ball and basketball hoop. The teams divide up on the two sides of a half court, forming two parallel lines. The player on the left gets the ball, dribbles to the basket, shoots and then passes the ball to the person in the position across from him in the first position on the right. The first player then runs to take his position at the end of that line, while the player who received the ball dribbles across the court to the player at the head of the left line, passes to him, and runs to the end of the left line. Continue until all have had a chance to shoot and then change the direction to the right for shooting.

Games *(cont.)*

Outdoor Games *(cont.)*

Basketball *(cont.)*

Horse

Equipment: basketball and court for each team—team size may vary

To play: Divide the class into as many groups as you have hoops. The first person on a team makes a shot, any shot. If the player misses, then he or she moves to the end of the line and it's the next person's turn. If a basket is made, then the person behind that shooter must make the same type of shot. If the second player makes the shot, then it's the next person's turn. The first person who misses a shot gets the letter H—on the way to spelling "Horse." The player who comes after a missed shot may make any type of shot. When the entire word "Horse" is spelled by any player, then that player is out. Play continues until there is only one player left. "Horse" also can be changed to "Rat" or "Elephant," etc., depending on the time and skill involved.

Kickball-Basketball

Equipment: a basketball court surrounded by lots of room and a kickball or soccer ball

To play: The object of this game is for the outfield team to make a basket before the player who is up runs around the edge of the basketball court to "home." Divide the class into two teams. Line one team up at the corner of the court, which becomes home plate. Play is like regular kickball, except the kicker runs all around the edges of the basketball court to score. The only way to get the runner out is if the outfield team brings the ball back to the court and makes a basket before the runner makes it around the court. Poor players can drop kick the ball; use two courts to run around if your class is just learning to shoot.

Number Basketball

Equipment: a basketball

To play: This game is similar to Steal the Bacon. Divide the class into two teams. The teacher bounces the ball in the center court and waits for a player to take it. Use basketball rules for safety.

Bean Bag Toss

Equipment: bean bags or other soft things to throw, such as sponges

To play: Divide your class into groups of about 10 students. Each group should have three bean bags. Children number themselves off and then form circles so that the numbers are not in order. The child who is number 1 throws to number 2 saying, "Two," while throwing the bean bag. Then number 2 throws the bean bag to number 3, calling "Three," etc. After the players have gotten the hang of it, add the second bean bag, and then the third. Once they have the idea, make it more complicated by calling out, "Shift." That's when everyone has to find a different place in the circle while keeping their numbers.

G

Games (cont.)

Outdoor Games (cont.)

Cone Kick-Down

Equipment: baseball diamond; four cones, one for each team

To play: Divide the class into four teams and number the players as for "Steal the Bacon." Line up on the baselines of a baseball field, one team on each baseline. Put the cones in the center of the diamond and then call out a number. The student from each team with that number leaves the line and runs around the outside of all the bases (and lines), back through his or her place in line, and into the center of the square, where he kicks down the cone. The first player to kick down the cone scores a point for his team.

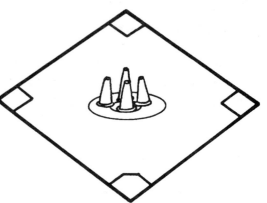

Dodge Ball

Equipment: one or two large rubber balls

> **General Rules**
> 1. Balls must be aimed below the waists of players.
> 2. No player, either inside or outside of the circle, may cross the line.
> 3. When a ball goes out of the playing area, only those players between whom it passed may retrieve it.

Regular Dodge Ball

Equipment: one large rubber ball and a large, marked circle

To play: Divide the class into four teams. Select one team to go inside the circle and direct the other teams to stand on the outside of the circle. Players on the outside must try to hit players on the inside with the ball; players on the inside must try to dodge the ball. When an inside player is hit, he or she is to join those on the outside to try to get their team out. Remind the hit players that the sooner the team is out, the sooner they get to be inside the circle again. In this way, all the children are playing all the time.

Double Dodge Ball

Equipment: two large rubber balls and a large, marked circle

To play: See regular dodge ball above, but use two balls instead of one for twice the fun!

G

Games (cont.)

Outdoor Games (cont.)

Dodge Ball (cont.)

Nation Dodge Ball

Equipment: one large rubber ball; a large, marked volleyball or basketball court

To play: Divide the class into two teams and direct each team to one side of the court. Select three players on each team to stand behind the opposite team's end of the court, the end zone. When the ball strikes a player on the opposite team, that player goes to the end zone to help his teammates. These three players are to catch the ball when it comes their way. They can then "sandwich" the opposing team to get them out. When the ball strikes the first three players, they are to replace the team members on the outside, who may now get a chance to dodge the ball inside the court. In this game, when an inside player drops the ball, he or she is out. But if a player catches the ball, he or she can use it to get someone out on the opposing team.

Jump Rope

Equipment: individual and large jump ropes

To play: Do not forget that besides building stamina (tell your boys that boxers religiously use them), jump ropes can be used to mark lines, jumped over in a class contest of "high jump," and used to mark distances in other jumping contests.

Kitty Wants a Corner

Equipment: four-square courts for every 5 to 8 students

Even fifth and sixth graders enjoy this game sometimes. Try assigning them to teach it to younger brothers or sisters as "homework."

To play: Divide children into as many groups as you have square courts, with at least five players on each team. (Volleyball courts work in a pinch.) Four of the players stand on the corners of the square and one player, "kitty," stands in the middle. Extra players line up outside a few feet away. The player in the middle goes to one corner person, saying, "Kitty wants a corner." (Older student can say "I want to rent a room.") The corner person replies, "Go to my next door neighbor." The person who is "kitty" then walks to the next person and repeats the process. This becomes fun as the players switch corners behind the "kitty's" back before kitty sees them. When one of the players loses a corner he or she either becomes the "kitty" or goes to the end of the line—if there is one.

G

Games *(cont.)*

Outdoor Games *(cont.)*

Pirate the Flag

Equipment: A field area about the size of three baseball diamonds to begin. (Once the students have learned the game, a larger field can be used.) The play area is best when marked off with cones. Although cones are expensive, they can be used for many different games, and they may be worth the investment if you are playing on an unmarked area. You will also need two 30 foot (9 meter) ropes to mark off two circles.

To play: Divide the field into halves. Designate a corner in each half as a "brig" and place a ball inside the roped-off circle. Then divide the class into two teams. Tell them that the object of the game is for each team to be the first to cross into the other team's territory, grab the ball, and escape with it to the other side. If a player is touched by an opposing team member while in that opposing team's territory, then he must go to the "brig" and stay there until one of his own untagged teammates frees him by touching him. Try to create the brig areas around a backstop or other barrier and require those in the brigs to keep a hand on the fence or other object until they are freed. Otherwise, it's just too easy for them to sneak back to their playing area!

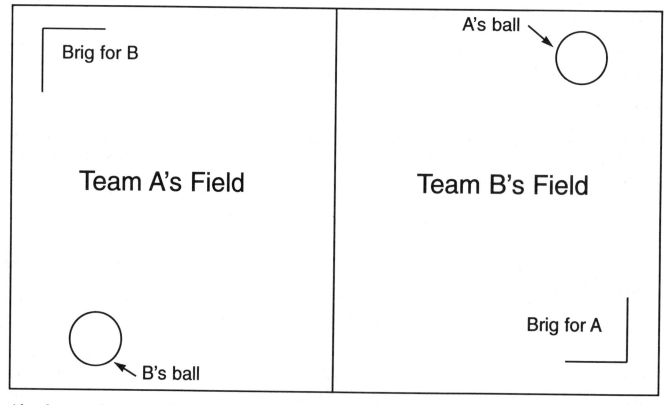

Also, be sure the roped-off areas for the balls are large enough so that two or three players can fit inside and be out of reach of the opposite team. Team B cannot step into Team A's roped-off area and vice versa. If this does occur, the errant player is considered out of bounds and goes to his own brig. This rule also applies to anyone who steps over the side or end lines.

#029 The Busy Teacher's Survival Guide   42   *© Teacher Created Materials, Inc.*

G

Games (cont.)

Outdoor Games (cont.)

Relay Races

Relay races are a good way to have students practice hopping, jumping, skipping, and listening to directions. Since each individual race is so short, give the winning team points. Also, have the winning team sit as soon as their relay is finished; it makes it easier to keep track of what's going on. Try some of the following variations.

Alligator: Teams line up in straight lines, each player in a squatting position with hands on the waist of the person in front of him or her. Teams play the relay to the finish, but the team must start over again if anyone stands up or the line becomes separated. Good for communication skills and cooperation.

Crab: Line teams up facing sideways. "Crab" runners get down on hands and feet and race to the end line and back, facing the same way while going up and back.

Over-Under: Line teams in straight lines about an arm's distance apart. The first person in line passes a ball under his legs to the next person who passes over his head to the next who passes under, etc. When the ball reaches the end of the line, the last person runs to the front and passes over, etc.

Soccer (Circle)

Equipment: a soccer ball and a marked circle

To play: The object of the game is to get the ball out of the circle. Divide the class into two teams and direct them to form one circle, all holding hands. Have students on team one hold their hands up so everyone can see where the teams begin and end. Throw the ball into the middle of the circle. The game begins as students try to kick the ball past the legs of the opposite team. A team gains a point only if the ball is kicked at a level below the waist; otherwise, the other team scores a point if the ball is kicked too hard or if it's kicked too high.

Squirrel and Foxes

Equipment: two bean bag "foxes" and one soft foam rubber "squirrel" ball

To play: The object of this game is to keep the "squirrel" away from the "foxes." Divide the class into three teams and have the teams sit in separate circles. Begin with the fox bean bags and squirrel ball in each circle. Bean bags may only be passed from hand to hand as students try to catch the squirrel ball by touching it with a bean bag. The squirrel ball may be thrown across the circle in an attempt to get away. When a fox touches the squirrel, the person holding the squirrel is out and leaves the circle. Play continues.

Outdoor Games *(cont.)*

Steal the Bacon

Equipment: an object such as a chalkboard eraser to use as the "bacon"

To play: Divide the class into two teams and place them into two lines facing each other. Assign each player a number. (If there is an extra player, then the last player on the other team gets two numbers.) Place the "bacon" between the lines. The teacher calls a number and the two players having that number race for the bacon. The bacon must not be hit or kicked out of position, but grabbed and run with all the way across the team's line. A point is scored if a player is tagged by the other player whose number was called or if the player can make it back to his own side. Be sure to keep track of the numbers you've already called with a pencil and paper.

Streets and Alleys

Equipment: no equipment needed for this game

To play: Choose three students: caller, cat, and mouse. The remaining students line up in neat rows and columns, their arms raised and touching. The caller faces away from the class. Starting at the opposite corners, the cat runs through the rows trying to catch the mouse without cutting through any line of students. At any time, the caller may shout, "Change!" and the class changes from rows to columns, or vice versa. Keep playing until the mouse is caught; the players then choose someone new to take their places.

Volleyball (Prisoner)

Equipment: netted volleyball court, volleyball.

To Play: Divide the class into two teams facing each other on the volleyball court. The player holding the ball says an opposing player's name and then throws the ball over the net. The ball is to be caught by any player before it touches the ground. If the ball is not caught, the player whose name was called goes outside the court to stand in line. The person in possession of the ball then calls out the name of a player on the opposing team and throws the ball back across the net. However, if a thrower would rather have one of his own team members come back into the game rather than get an opposing team member out he or she may call out, "Prisoner!" The first person in line gets to come back in.

Other rules: (1) If the ball touches the net, lands outside the court lines, or the thrower forgets to call a name, the thrower is out and must stand in line; (2) After catching a ball, the thrower may take only three steps; (3) The person who catches the ball may not pass it to anyone else to throw.

Games *(cont.)*

Indoor Games

Not all these games are for rainy days only. Many can be used to review math, social studies facts, etc. Please look them over when you want to add a little fun to a dull day or when your students are already restless or noisy. Many of these games have a noise penalty attached, so they can actually be used to calm students down. Reward winners of these games with a treat or a ribbon of some sort for playing well, for being a good sport, or for cooperation.

Four Corners

Before the game begins, number the corners one through four. One student faces the chalkboard with his eyes closed, and he or she gets to call the numbers. At the beginning of the game, all students go to the corners of their choice. The caller then calls out the number of a corner, and all students in that corner return to their seats. Remaining children all move to a new corner, and the caller again calls out a number. Play continues until only one child is left, and that child will be the new caller.

As more and more players sit down, there may be a corner without any students in it. If that happens, the students do not move, but instead a new corner is called, the students in that corner sit down, and play continues.

Seven Up

Seven students are chosen to stand at the head of the class. All others sit at their desks with their foreheads squarely on the desks (so there is no peeking under their arms) and have one hand out on their desks with a thumb up. A person who is "it" walks quietly by, gently touches a thumb, and then returns to the front of the class. When all the students from the front of the class have chosen a person, they line up and you—or a designated student—calls, "Heads up, seven up." The seven people whose thumbs have been touched stand and then take turns guessing who chose them. If they are right, then that person sits down, and the person who guessed then stands at the end of the line of players. After everyone chosen has had a chance to guess, the players who are still standing say the name of the person they chose.

Indoor Games *(cont.)*

20 Questions

This game is good for subject review. A student thinks of an item. Students then ask questions which can be answered "yes" or "no." The student who guesses the item then chooses the next item to be guessed. It takes a bit of practice to get the hang of this game, but it is well worth it for many subject areas.

Bang!

Use this game to review multiplication facts and to practice listening skills. To begin, students sit on their desks. You decide on a number; five is a good choice for learning to play this game. The students begin counting, each saying a number, but student numbers five, ten, and fifteen will say, "Bang!" instead of "five," "ten," or "fifteen," and so forth. In other words, the count will be, "One . . . two . . . three . . . four . . . bang! Six . . . seven . . . eight . . . nine . . . bang!" If a child makes a mistake or talks out of turn, then the count goes back to one for the next child, and the student who made the mistake sits down in his or her chair. Once they learn to play this game with multiples of five, try other multiples. For variety, students can substitute "Pop!" or "Ding!" for multiples.

Chief

Chief is good for getting students to pay attention. Seat students in a large circle while one child leaves the room. One of the students in the circle is chosen to be chief. The player sent outside is brought back in again to the center of the circle. The chief will begin a movement, and all the others sitting around the circle will follow it. After a while, the chief will vary the movement, making the difference as big as he can, and all others in the circle will change their movement to match. The chief then changes again and yet again. The person in the center gets three chances to guess who the chief is. If the guess is right, then the chief goes out of the room. If the guess is not correctly made, the chief reveals himself and gets to choose a new person to be it. After that person leaves the room, the old chief also gets to choose a new chief, and play continues.

G

Games *(cont.)*

Indoor Games *(cont.)*

Eraser Tag

Equipment: two chalkboard erasers or bean bags

To play: Somehow this game always winds up pitting boys against girls; you can either go with tradition or have mixed teams. Two chosen team members stand in opposite corners with chalkboard erasers on the tops of their heads. A caller facing the blackboard calls out who is to chase whom. The chaser chases the other student around the room. If the chalkboard eraser is touched or falls off, the other team gets the point. The fun comes in when the child facing the chalkboard calls out—at any time and varying the frequency—"Change!" The caller can keep a tally of the score on the chalkboard.

Hangman

This game can be used to review current vocabulary words.

I'm Going to New York

This is a game of listening and memory skills. The object of the game is to make a long, alphabetical list of items the students will take with them on a trip to New York, each student adding an item in alphabetical order from A to Z and then repeating all the items named before his or her turn. So, by the time play reaches student number four, he or she will say, "I'm going to New York, and I'm going to take a dog, a cup, a ball, and an apple." Play continues through the alphabet and around the circle. When a child cannot remember what comes next, he or she drops out of the circle and play continues from that point. Make this game relevant with variations, such as, "I'm going on safari," with students listing animals, or "I'm going to the American Revolution," with students listing historic figures and events.

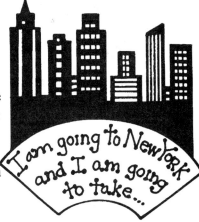

Inside Baseball

This game is great for reviewing a variety of subjects. Decide where each "base" will be in your class. (It is more fun to play if the children get to move around.) Divide the class into two teams. You may want to let each team choose its name and write that on the chalkboard with "runs" and "outs" listed under it. As the first batter comes up, he or she may ask for a single, double, triple, or home run to designate the difficulty of the question he or she would like to answer. Take into account the student's ability when you "throw" a question at him or her. If the child gets a "hit," then he or she gets to go to the corresponding base. If, on the other hand, the child gets an "out," his or her play is ended until it is his or her turn again, and you can use the question with the next player who asks for the same level of difficulty.

Indoor Games *(cont.)*

Inside Baseball *(cont.)*

When students get to home base, they score a point for their team. Students could make up packs of cards for you to use as questions in various subject areas, or you may have questions prepared ahead of time. Another idea is to use a set of store-bought cards.

Pipeline Relay

Equipment: plenty of tape and a sheet of paper for each child (Scratch paper will do along with a paper ball— a crumpled half sheet of paper.)

To play: This game is plain fun. Begin by having each student make a paper tube. Divide the class into teams, have the teams stand in rows, and give the leader a paper ball. The ball is passed from the front to the back of the line through the paper tubes. If the ball drops or is touched, then it is returned to the front of the line. The winning team is the first one that has had everyone at the front.

Silent Ball

Equipment: soft foam ball

To play: This game is a quiet classic. Begin with all students seated on their desks. A soft sponge or Koosh ball is tossed from one student to another with no talking allowed. Players who drop the ball, throw too hard, or talk must sit in their seats. Continue play until only one student is sitting on his or her desk.

Snakes and Bees

Equipment: red and black checkers or similar playing pieces

To play: Divide the class into two teams—the "rattlesnakes" and the "bumble bees." The snakes must find a red checker, the bees a black one. One member from each team goes out of the room while a member of the opposite team hides the checker in such a way that it really can be found, i.e., leave it exposed a bit or out in a clever nook or cranny. When the two players enter the room, their teammates try to let them know where their team's checker is by the bees buzzing when the bumble bee is close to the black checker and the snakes hissing when the rattlesnake is close to the red one.

G

Games *(cont.)*

Indoor Games *(cont.)*

Spell It Backwards

Students needs to concentrate for this game. Players sit on their desks. Give the first player a simple word to spell. He or she spells one letter of the word going backwards and then the next in line gives the next-to-last letter, etc. If a mistake is made, that player sits down or gets a point against him, and the play continues.

States Relay

Equipment: a large wall map

To play: Use this game to review not only the states but also countries, geographical features, etc. Divide students into two teams and line them up in front of a large map. Call out the name of something you want the students to identify. The first student to touch it with a finger earns a point for his or her team. After a point has been scored, the students move to the end of the line, and the next two players take a turn.

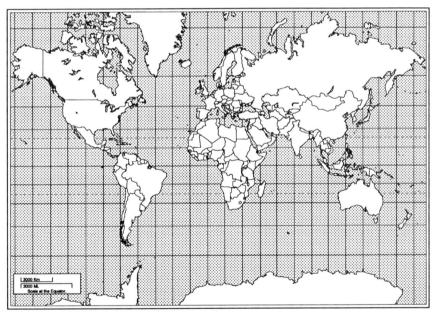

Purchased Board Games

Many students do not have board games at home, and this is a shame. Your school may have money available for checkers or chess pieces and boards, but you might also try looking at swap meets and thrift stores for used ones. Older students can also try their hands at making their own board games. It's a great project for a rainy day!

G

Grading

Whatever your philosophy about grading, the most important point is that children and their parents need to know their progress. Report cards should never be a complete surprise. Be sure to provide graded feedback on a regular basis. Some students do not have a clue as to what the different grades mean, so make a poster and keep it posted above the chalkboard.

Grades

A = Absolutely wonderful

B = Better than most

C = Could have done better

D = Didn't learn much

F = Failed to learn anything

You might want to add "D.O.," which stands for "Do Over." This gives students a chance to correct their work and really learn, which is the whole point.

For grades to be valuable, students need to have notice if they are not doing well in something while they still have an opportunity to improve. Midterm evaluations or progress reports distributed in the middle of the marking period are important checkpoints for both students and parents. They are reminders that there is still time to make necessary changes. Parents and students need to know how they can get help if students are not as successful as they hoped, so the teacher should be ready with suggestions if a request is made. If your school does not already have an established form to use for midterm evaluation, reproduce the form below (or use it as a sample) and distribute it at the appropriate time.

Midterm Progress Report for

_____
(Student's Name)

Subject(s):	Average	Above Average	Needs Improvement	Comments:

_____   _____
(Parent's Signature)   (Teacher's Signature)

G

Group Work

Group work provides students with valuable experience in cooperative learning. A common complaint from both teachers and students is about the one student who is just along for the ride while the others do all the work. To alleviate this problem, at the end of any extended group work, have each student anonymously grade the work the group has done and assign a grade to everyone in that group, including him or herself. Use this to help you evaluate each student. In this way, students get the grade that they earned.

The culmination of group work might be to have students do individual work, a group presentation to which everyone must contribute, or a test so that you can discover who was really paying attention and learning.

Grouping

Groups of four are best for many activities, but if you must have them, groups of three or five are workable. Consider odd-numbered groups for activities in which a deciding vote may be necessary. Mix sexes, cultures, and ability levels for most activities. The exception is when students form their own reading groups to work together on a book of their choosing, but even then there is usually a mix.

Students should be open to sitting and working with all types of students, but in reality there are individual students with whom it may be difficult to work for a variety of reasons. Especially for long-term group work, you might try asking the students to privately write down the names of three to five students with whom they would like to work and create groups on this basis as much as possible.

Another way to form temporary groups is to use a deck of cards. Pull out as many sets of cards as you wish to create in groups of four—for instance, if you have twenty-eight students to form into seven groups, then pull all the cards from aces to sevens from the deck. Ask students to choose a card from your new deck. All students holding a four are in one group, all those holding a six are in another group, etc.

Change groups and seating arrangements at a maximum time of six weeks—the students will need a change of scenery and a chance to know everyone better, and you will find, as an added benefit, that the room is quieter for awhile.

H

Height Chart

Students love to see their changes in height during the year, and if you teach them how to measure, the whole class can be measured in under 10 minutes. (Call students up by rows or groups while the rest of the students do art or something else they can be equally involved in.) You'll need 1/2" (1.25 cm) tagboard and about 10 different colors of marking pens. Leave about four inches (10 cm) at the left margin and then mark the tagboard at every inch (2.5 cm) and label each month of the school year across the top. Have kids take their shoes off, stand in line and choose a pen and then stand straight under the name of the appropriate month. If the color of pen they chose is too close to someone else who has the same color, ask the students to change colors. Then write their names at their heights in the margin at the left and put dots on the lines of the appropriate months at the same heights. Repeat this process monthly, making sure that each student chooses the same color of pen each time.

Homework

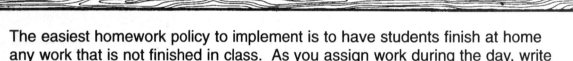

The easiest homework policy to implement is to have students finish at home any work that is not finished in class. As you assign work during the day, write the assignment on the chalkboard. Erase the assignments the next day as the papers are collected. This serves many purposes:

1. The children have a list of what has been assigned. Urge the students to check the board before they go home to make sure that their work has been completed or that they have the required books and papers needed to complete their work.

2. You can copy the assignments after school so that you can refer to them when a student is absent and easily fill in the students' Weekly Reports (see pages 129–130).

3. You can make sure that all assigned work is corrected and collected the day it is due.

Occasionally, you can assign work to the students so that their parents can see what you are doing in class or send home math puzzle problems which are enjoyed by most students, and some parents.

Homework *(cont.)*

However, do remember that some parents work long hours and that others may not have the academic background to do school work.

When assigning reports, write down the requirements, due date, and how much point value is assigned for each part of the report, such as the cover, table of contents, spelling, maps, etc. Then ask each child to take the paper home and have the bottom signed and returned. This not only helps parents keep their students on track, but it makes it easier for you to grade their work when it does come in.

Homework Passes

Students will definitely work for these! Use homework passes permitting a homework free night if a child earns an "A" on a very hard test or does really well on something special. When you hand out a pass, state the subject for which the student may use it. After all, if he or she gets a high mark on a history test, chances are that missing one work assignment will not severely affect the student's overall history knowledge.

Design a homework pass on your computer or by hand or use the sample below. Sign it before reproducing the pass. You can place about eight passes on a page, one for each major subject plus a blank for minor subjects. Add a graphic from a rubber stamp, advertisement, newspaper, etc., to each pass. Keep the passes in a file box on your desk. When a child earns a pass, just fill in his or her name and staple it onto the award-winning paper.

Congratulations!

_____

has earned a homework pass in

_____ .

_____
Teacher's Signature

L

Labeling

You need to put your name on everything! As you take material you have purchased out of its bag, write your name on it. Write it in big letters on the front of your activity books. On books for the class, write it on the edge of the pages at the top. This way if the book goes home or to another teacher's class, it is easily identified and returned. You might think about getting a stamp with your name on it—it saves time.

Laminating

Find out if your school or district can do this for you. Laminate every poster you make or buy if you can. Things last much longer as the edges do not tear, fading is slower, and they cannot be smudged by you or the children.

Lesson Plan Book

Keep your plans in a three-ring notebook instead of the usual spiral one available in educational supply stores or provided by the district. It will be much easier to have many materials close at hand, and if you make a master copy of lesson plans which includes subjects, recesses, library time, etc., at the beginning of the year, you will save at least 15 minutes of work each week.

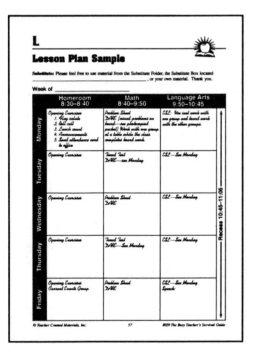

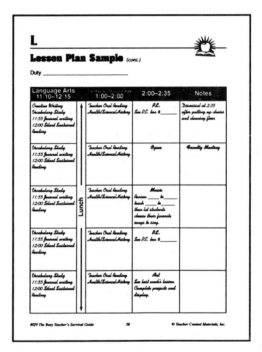

The sample lesson plan on pages 57–58 does not follow the current theme plan required by many school districts, but it may still prove useful for those in-between times not devoted to theme teaching. If you are a beginning teacher, you may feel more comfortable beginning the year with a traditional plan and attempting to use themes later in the year. Perhaps you can start with a theme for a single day and then stretch one out for a week. Themes can also be used for part of the day, such as the language arts block. A flexible approach to planning is best in order to suit the needs of you and your students.

L

Lesson Plan Book *(cont.)*

In your lesson plan book, use tab divisions labeled as follows. Two sets of reproducible tabs are provided on page 56. A blank set of tabs in also provided.

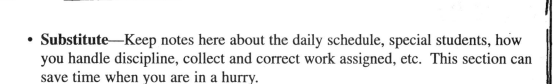

- **Substitute**—Keep notes here about the daily schedule, special students, how you handle discipline, collect and correct work assigned, etc. This section can save time when you are in a hurry.

- **Lesson Plans**—See pages 57–58 for sample lesson plans. Blank lesson plan forms are provided on pages 59–60.

- **Lists**—Include ideas for speeches, creative writing, PE, etc. Check ideas off as you use them, or mark your way down the list with sticky notes.

- **Schedules**—Include yard duty, library and computer schedules, etc. (It's nice to have this handy if you ever need to call another teacher to trade times.)

- **Audio-Visual (A.V.)**—Keep a list of computer programs available in the lab and in your room, as well as lists of district films and records, materials that you use for themes, etc.

- **School/District Bulletins**—Include a list of teachers and their room numbers so you can send student messengers to the right person (and spell the name right, too). This is also a good place to include important district bulletins.

- **Teacher Association**—Keep handy a copy of your rights, responsibilities for reporting child abuse, lists of union representatives, teacher association obligations, etc.

- **Faculty Meetings**—Depending on the amount of information passed out at faculty meetings, you may wish to combine this with School Bulletins.

- **Supplies**—Maintain a list of items both to order and on order. Keep a wish list in case the school or district surprises you with funds.

- **Student Information**—Include the language spoken in the home, with whom the child lives, home and work addresses, and phone numbers.

- **Miscellaneous**—Anything that does not fit the above categories is placed here.

Always put your lesson plan book in an obvious place when you leave for the night. You never know when you might have an emergency or an illness and not be able to go in the next day.

L

Lesson Plan Book Tabs

Substitute Information	Lesson Plans	Lists
Schedules	Audio-Visual	School/District Bulletins
Teacher Association	Faculty Meetings	Supplies
Student Information	Miscellaneous	

Substitute Information	Lesson Plans	Lists
Schedules	Audio-Visual	School/District Bulletins
Teacher Association	Faculty Meetings	Supplies
Student Information	Miscellaneous	

L

Lesson Plan Sample

Substitute: Please feel free to use material from the Substitute Folder, the Substitute Box located
_____ , or your own material. Thank you.

Week of _____

	Homeroom 8:30–8:40	Math 8:40–9:50	Language Arts 9:50–10:45	
Monday	Opening Exercises 1. Flag salute 2. Roll call 3. Lunch count 4. Announcements 5. Send attendance card to office	Problem Sheet DARE (mixed problems on board—see photocopied packet) Work with one group at a table while the class completes board work.	ESL: Use seat work with one group and board work with the other groups.	Recess 10:45–11:05
Tuesday	Opening Exercises	Timed Test DARE—see Monday	ESL—See Monday	
Wednesday	Opening Exercises	Problem Sheet DARE	ESL—See Monday	
Thursday	Opening Exercises	Timed Test DARE—See Monday	ESL—See Monday	
Friday	Opening Exercises Current Events Group	Problem Sheet DARE	ESL—See Monday Speech:	

L

Lesson Plan Sample *(cont.)*

Duty _____

Language Arts 11:10–12:15	1:00 Mike and Markus to RSP 1:00–2:00	2:00–2:35	Notes
Creative Writing Vocabulary Study 11:55 Journal writing 12:00 Silent Sustained Reading	*Teacher Oral Reading Health/Science/History*	**P.E.** *See P.E. box #_____*	*Dismissal at 2:35 after putting up chairs and cleaning floor*
Vocabulary Study 11:55 Journal writing 12:00 Silent Sustained Reading	*Teacher Oral Reading Health/Science/History*	**Open**	**Faculty Meeting**
Vocabulary Study 11:55 Journal writing 12:00 Silent Sustained Reading	*Teacher Oral Reading Health/Science/History*	**Music** *Review ____ to____ teach ____ to____ then let students choose their favorite songs to sing.*	
Vocabulary Study 11:55 Journal writing 12:00 Silent Sustained Reading	*Teacher Oral Reading Health/Science/History*	**P.E.** *See P.E. box #_____*	
Vocabulary Study 11:55 Journal writing 12:00 Silent Sustained Reading	*Teacher Oral Reading Health/Science/History*	**Art** *See last week's lesson. Complete projects and display.*	

(Lunch — vertical column between Language Arts and 1:00–2:00 columns)

Lesson Plan Form

Substitute: Please feel free to use material from the Substitute Folder, the Substitute Box located
_____ , or your own material. Thank you.

Week of _____

Monday				
Tuesday				
Wednesday				
Thursday				
Friday				

L

Lesson Plan Form *(cont.)*

Duty _____

L

Letters to Parents

Following is a sample of a letter to send home to parents the first week of school. You may wish to delete or include ideas that fit your plan for the year. Build a solid home-school relationship by communicating frequently with parents.

Dear Parents,

Today your child is bringing home something important for you to see—the Home Reading Chart. All students become better readers by practicing reading. For this reason, I require that students spend at least one-half hour reading silently each day, fifteen minutes in class and fifteen minutes at home. They may read anything but textbooks, because the point is for them to learn to love reading all kinds of material. Reading aloud to you or to a younger brother or sister is also a good and helpful idea. Please provide a quiet environment for reading and sign the chart nightly.

On _____ , your child will bring home a "Weekly Report" and will continue to do so each week of the year. If the report has negative information on it, please discuss it with your child and then plan to see me so that we can work together to take care of the problem.

I rarely assign homework, but I do ask students to complete their classwork assignments at home. Your child should have had time to ask questions and get help during class, but if not, he or she can call his or her "Study Buddy," to be chosen tomorrow. (If you do not want your child to participate in this activity, please send a note requesting that your telephone number not be given out.)

Should your child need more help, he or she can stay in at recess or after school, or come to school in the morning between 7 and 8 o'clock.

Work missed during an absence must be made up. Students need to check with their study buddies and with me upon returning to class. A student absent for several days needs to make special arrangements to catch up.

I would also like to have as many parents as possible visit the class during the year. If you have time to tutor students or to share one of your own special skills, please let me know. The more children see that their parents care about—and get involved in—their school, the better they do as students.

Please contact me with any questions. I hope this is a great year for us all!

Sincerely,

_____   _____
Teacher's Signature   Parent's Signature

Letters to Parents *(cont.)*

Conference Request/English

To the Parents of _____

Dear Parents,

Your child is having difficulty:

_____ turning completed work in on time.

_____ following rules.

I would very much like to talk to you about this problem. Please fill out the bottom of this form so that I may see you as soon as possible and we can find a way to help your child improve.

Sincerely,

_____

- -

Child's name: _____

Please schedule an appointment for me at:

_____ 6:30 A.M.   _____ 2:45 P.M.

_____ 7:00 A.M.   _____ 3:15 P.M.

_____ 7:30 A.M.   _____ Before 6:30 A.M. at_____

_____ 8:00 A.M.   _____ (other)

_____ I cannot see you at this time.

_____ Please call me at home tonight at this number: _____

Parent's Signature:

_____

Letters to Parents *(cont.)*

Conference Request/Spanish

Para los Padres de_____

Queridos Padres,

Su hijo/hija esta teniendo problemas:

_____ terminando su trabajo de escuela a tiempo.

_____ siguiendo las reglas de la escuela.

Yo nesecito a hablar con Uds. sobre esta problema. Por favor llene abajo de esta forma para ver de que forma se le puede ayudar a sus hijo o hija.

Gracias,

_____

- -

Nombre de estudiante: _____

Por favor, ponga que hora es buena para venir a verme:

____ 6:30 A.M.   ____ 2:45 P.M.

____ 7:00 A.M.   ____ 3:15 P.M.

____ 7:30 A.M.   ____ antes de 6:30 a las_____

____ 8:00 A.M.   ____ (otro)

____ No puede verla en dichas horas.

____ Hableme por favor a casa. Mi numero de telefono: _____

Firma de Padres:

_____

Dear Parents,

Attached to this letter you will find your child's timed multiplication test. Students take a timed test every day in math so that they can learn the facts and quickly come up with the answers. Multiplication facts should be learned in the third grade and mastered by the fifth grade. Your child must pass this test in _____minutes by the next report card in order to earn a _____ or above in math.

Using flash cards is a good way to learn the multiplication facts. Pull out all of the "twos" multiplication facts and practice with them. After these are learned, pull out the "threes" and work only with them. When these are learned, combine the twos and threes and practice both sets of facts. Then work with only the "fours," master them, and combine again. Do this with all of the facts. Your child may work alone part of the time, but an adult needs to work with him for at least 10 minutes every night. Thank you for helping your child become a better student!

_____

Teacher's Signature

L

Letters to Parents *(cont.)*

Home Reading Chart

Every student must read 15 minutes each night from Monday through Thursday.

Date	Title of book or magazine	Number of pages read	Parent's signature

Manipulatives

Before passing out any manipulatives, be very clear about their purpose and how they are and are not to be used in the room. At a recent seminar, the leader offered two simple rules: "Keep it on the table. Put it in the bag." Remove the materials from students who misuse them and tell them they can have another chance next time; have an alternative assignment ready for these students to keep them occupied while you continue your lesson.

Any time you hand out new manipulatives (or art materials or anything novel), allow some playtime so that students will be more apt to listen to the lesson when you are ready to teach. Of course, if the students become very involved in their play, throw your plans out the window and allow them to learn on their own for awhile.

A math manipulative worth its weight in gold is centimeter cubes. They are good for counting, adding, subtracting, place value, multiplying, ratios, patterns, etc. Do not be without them if at all possible. Ask your resource teacher if there are any cubes you can borrow or, better yet, can be purchased for you. There are interlocking cubes and plain cubes; try both styles in your classroom to see which you like better before ordering any.

If you need play coins and money for math, check the resource books that come with most mathematics kits before you purchase any. It is much less expensive to run these off and have the students cut them out.

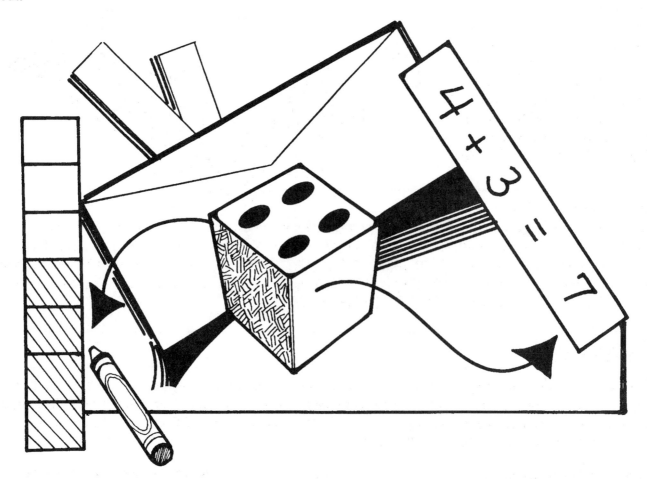

M

Manipulatives *(cont.)*

There are three more math manipulatives you should not do without. One is a straight edge—a ruler. You'll be surprised at how many kids do not know how to use a ruler for measurement or for drawing straight edges. For safety reasons, try to get a ruler without a metal edge. If you teach in the primary grades, get rulers marked by the quarter inch; for older students, regular rulers with both English and metric systems are better.

Another mandatory manipulative is a good compass. Do not be penny wise and pound foolish when it comes to purchasing compasses. Choose ones that will hold a variety of writing utensils and that will hold up to the rigors of classroom use. (See the Dale Seymour resource on page 97.)

The last golden manipulative is number tiles. You can use them for place value, for logic puzzles, for children to show you their understanding, etc. A classroom set costs about thirty dollars, but you can make your own number tiles by going to a tile store and buying one-inch (2.5 cm) squares which come in sheets of 100 for about $3.00. Use a permanent marker and a ruler to mark the bottoms so that students do not confuse the sixes and nines. After numbering the tiles, you can get the backing off by soaking them in warm, soapy water. Rinse and let dry, then bag each set.

Any small manipulatives can be separated into plastic bags for groups so you do not have to divide them each time. Buy heavy bags—they are expensive but last longer and so are worth it. Before you put the manipulatives in, use a hole punch to punch a hole. If your hole punch doesn't work well, stick an index card behind the bag and punch through them both. The bags will last longer that way, as the children won't be able to pop them. They also will be flat and, therefore, easier to store.

Masters

With copy machines turning out better and better copies, it makes sense to mark your original masters with correction fluid "X" on the upper right-hand corner. Also, if you have trouble getting a clear copy because the machine is picking up type from both sides of the master, put black paper behind your original before making your copies. It works!

Math

Board Work

Talk through problems as you work them on the board in front of your class. Ask students for rules or answers before writing the steps to solving problems. It gives the children practice in listening to and repeating steps. When the children lack motivation, allow them to shout or even whisper answers in order to wake them up!

Paper Format

At the beginning of the year, show students how you want them to format their math papers with name, date, assignment, and an answer column, if possible. Answer columns can save hours of work; just line up three or four papers and check them all at once! Always ask students to show their computations; if a student has made a lot of mistakes, you can easily find the incorrect problems, look them over to find out why the student got them wrong, and help him correct the problem.

Kate Johnson APRIL 23,			Math Test
			ANSWERS
1. 10 x 3 30	2. 6 x 3 18	3. 7 x 8	1. 30
			2. 18
			3.
			4.
4. 3 x 5	5. 6 x 9	6. 7 x 5	5.
			6.
			7.
			8.
7. 1 x 8	8. 5 x 4	9. 2 x 5	9.

Have students check their papers together as a class on the day they are due. If you have the students bring up their papers themselves by group or row, you can easily see who didn't get it done or who needs help, as well as pull out the papers with a lot of mistakes. After explaining and assigning the day's task, you can work individually or in small groups with those students who need help. Of course, if the children are working together in groups with only one paper turned in from the group, you will have to do your checking by touring the room, which, of course, you should be doing anyway.

Facts Drill

Give your students timed math fact quizzes at least twice a week at the beginning of class, depending on the grade level you are teaching and the children's skills. Despite the fact that it is not in vogue to drill students on facts, most veteran teachers feel that students need to know the basic facts of addition, subtraction, multiplication, and division—it takes too long for them to get anywhere if they do not have these at their fingertips by fifth and sixth grades! There are many books of practice drills that you can get at educational supply stores.

Facts Drill *(cont.)*

Give timed tests daily if multiplication facts are being introduced. Start with ones, just so the children can get their first happy faces or stars on the chart. (See below.) Then give only twos, then threes, etc. After they can do them singly, give them a test with all the facts mixed on it. They should be able to do it in five minutes.

Facts Chart

Keep all of the timed test records on a chart hung in the room. This encourages the students to study. They can also see which test they need to take and pass. Offer an award (see page 19) for each test they pass; perhaps have the students clap for each other when the awards are presented. Let the parents know about this classroom activity; see the sample letter on page 64.

Have two versions of each test and run them off on colored copy paper: addition in green, subtraction in yellow, multiplication in blue, and division in buff. Create a laminated answer sheet for each test paper and keep the answers in the front of your lesson plan book. (Run a fat red marking pen down the left edge of the second version of the answer sheet of each test so it's easy to find.) You won't need to use the answer sheets very often if you use the top student's paper to correct the others.

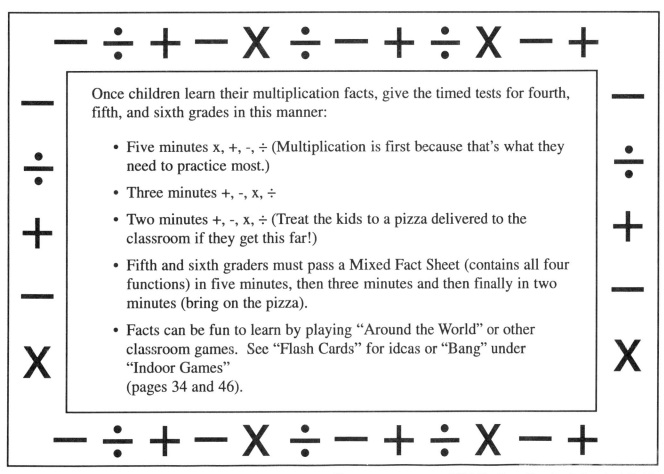

Once children learn their multiplication facts, give the timed tests for fourth, fifth, and sixth grades in this manner:

- Five minutes x, +, -, ÷ (Multiplication is first because that's what they need to practice most.)

- Three minutes +, -, x, ÷

- Two minutes +, -, x, ÷ (Treat the kids to a pizza delivered to the classroom if they get this far!)

- Fifth and sixth graders must pass a Mixed Fact Sheet (contains all four functions) in five minutes, then three minutes and then finally in two minutes (bring on the pizza).

- Facts can be fun to learn by playing "Around the World" or other classroom games. See "Flash Cards" for ideas or "Bang" under "Indoor Games" (pages 34 and 46).

Math *(cont.)*

Flash Cards for Fact Families

Make or buy flash cards which have the answers on them and then have students use index cards or their hand to cover up numbers in the set of facts so students can learn the related fact families. Try making flash cards with the multiplicands and product in a triangle formation to make seeing this relationship even easier.

Over the Hill Subtraction

For those students who cannot seem to master subtraction facts for numbers 1 through 20, teach them the "Over the Hill" method. Assuming that the students know the subtraction facts from one to ten and from ten to twenty, try showing them how to put both family facts together by writing the number 10 halfway "over the hill." They can then subtract the difference between the subtrahend and 10 and write it down and then subtract the difference between 10 and the minuend, and write it down to create an addition problem. Now, if they add those two differences, the students will find the answer to the problem.

$$
\begin{array}{c}
6 \diagup 16 \\
+1 \diagdown {}^{10} - 9 \\
\hline
7
\end{array}
\qquad
\begin{array}{c}
4 \diagup 14 \\
+2 \diagdown {}^{10} - 8 \\
\hline
6
\end{array}
\qquad
\begin{array}{c}
3 \diagup 13 \\
+3 \diagdown {}^{10} - 7 \\
\hline
6
\end{array}
$$

Learning Multiplication and Other Math Facts

Students in third grade can begin multiplying numbers sequentially, but in grades four through six, you can begin the year with the whole class on daily timed tests. Start with five-minute timed multiplication tests and then move on to addition, subtraction, and division. Then speed up the students to do their facts in three minutes and then two-minutes. Be sure to reward the students who can pass the two-minute test, perhaps with a gift certificate for an ice cream cone from a local shop.

If students have been given a reasonable amount of time to learn their math facts but are still woefully behind, send home a letter to parents asking them to make or purchase multiplication flash cards and to follow your method for learning.

M

Math *(cont.)*

Finger Facts for Sixes and Eights

For these facts, students can use their fingers. Tell students that the palm of their hand counts as "5" and to add that to the number of fingers they have held up. For example, "7" will resemble the palm and finger position in diagram A.

Use your fingers to calculate the number of tens and ones in the multiplication problem by adding the number of fingers which are down for the ones and adding the number of fingers which are up for the tens. For example, for the problem 6 x 8, if students use one hand to show "6" and the other to show "8," the number of fingers up—the tens—is equal to "4" and the number of fingers down—the ones—is equal to "8." The answer, then, is 48. (See diagram B.)

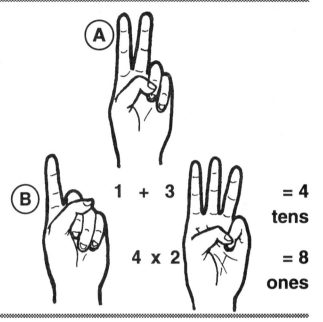

Finger Facts for Nines

To use fingers for nines, begin by having students put their hands up. Then, counting from left to right, find the finger that represents the number by which they wish to multiply 9 and lower it. Ask them to add up the number of fingers to the left of the lowered finger to find the number of tens in the answer and to add up the number of fingers to the right of the lowered finger to find the number of ones in the answer. For example, in multiplying 4 x 9, the fourth finger from the left goes down. The number of fingers to the left of the lowered finger—the tens—is "3," and the number of fingers to the right of the lowered finger— the ones—is "6." The answer, then, is 36.

Fact Ladder

Show students the "Nifty Nines Fact Ladder" on page 72. Nines form such a pattern that the number of tens in the product is always one less than the number by which you multiplied nine. Plus, the numbers in the product will always add up to nine.

Math *(cont.)*

Fact Ladder *(cont.)*

Nifty Nines

9 x 2 = 18
2 − 1 = 1 and
1 + 8 = 9
9 x 3 = 27
3 − 1 = 2 and
2 + 7 = 9
9 x 4 = 36
4 − 1 = 3 and
3 + 6 = 9
9 x 5 = 45
5 − 1 = 4 and
4 + 5 = 9
etc.

For the nines you can also have students multiply by 10 instead and then subtract the number they are multiplying. For example, rather than multiplying 9 x 3, multiply 10 x 3, which equals 30, and subtract 3 to get the desired answer of 27.

Computation

Many children do not understand what they are actually doing when they compute. If you do not believe that, ask them. Ask them anyway—it makes them think, and it's interesting to get their answers. Just say, for example, "What is addition?" Then stand back and listen to the show.

If they truly do not understand the operation of addition, tell them that addition is combining, that subtraction is separating, that multiplication is combining like amounts, or adding the same amount over and over, and that division is separating things into groups. Word problems should not be introduced until these concepts are understood. Try a few days of just posing word problems to the children aloud and having them tell you what the operation should be with hand signals held at chest height so if they are wrong no one else knows but you. In this way you can instantly see who still needs help with the concepts.

Math *(cont.)*

Teaching New Methods

With any new method you teach your students in math, make sure they all understand it then give them four homework problems where they must use the new method. Do this for three days in a row, with the added stipulation that on the last day they must teach someone at home how to do it and must have that person sign the homework paper. After those three days, you needn't require that they use the method again, but the new methods are usually so much easier that most students will continue to use them.

Column Addition Using Tick Marks

Many students have difficulty carrying numbers in their heads as the amounts get over twenty. With the "tick method," children write the sum down each time they get to ten or over by writing down the digit in the ones column and crossing out the last digit which made them go over ten. They then add the digit they wrote down to the next digit in the column. Repeat, writing down the ones digit and crossing out when necessary. At the end of the column they just count up the number of digits they crossed out and carry this to the next column.

Samples:

$$
\begin{array}{r}
4,985 \\
7,947 \\
3,652 \\
9,889 \\
\hline
26,473
\end{array}
\qquad
\begin{array}{r}
4,985 \\
7,947 \\
3,652 \\
+\,9,889 \\
\hline
26,473
\end{array}
\qquad
\begin{array}{r}
6,223 \\
8,778 \\
9,531 \\
+\,7,547 \\
\hline
32,079
\end{array}
\qquad
\begin{array}{r}
6,223 \\
8,778 \\
9,531 \\
+\,7,547 \\
\hline
32,079
\end{array}
$$

Recognizing "Borrowing"

For students who are just being introduced to what was once known as borrowing, or for older students who are having trouble, the problem often lies in their inability to think whether the subtraction problem is possible or not. If what they see is not possible, they just take the smaller digit from the larger no matter where it is, so first they need practice in just looking at the problem. Make up problems like this; the students write a "Y" for "yes" if it's possible to do the problem.

$$
\begin{array}{c}
8 \\
-7 \\
\hline
N
\end{array}
\qquad
\begin{array}{c}
8 \\
-5 \\
\hline
Y
\end{array}
\qquad
\begin{array}{c}
9 \\
-4 \\
\hline
Y
\end{array}
\qquad
\begin{array}{c}
8 \\
-3 \\
\hline
N
\end{array}
\qquad
\begin{array}{c}
7 \\
-5 \\
\hline
Y
\end{array}
\qquad
\begin{array}{c}
9 \\
-6 \\
\hline
N
\end{array}
\qquad
\begin{array}{c}
9 \\
-3 \\
\hline
Y
\end{array}
$$

Math *(cont.)*

Subtraction Using the Compensation Method

For harder subtraction problems, use the English compensation method. Instead of changing the numbers, just do two "compensations"—putting the ten value in the top row, and adding a value of one to the next number on the bottom left.

$$
\begin{array}{r}
4,6\overset{1}{7}\overset{1}{3} \\
- \overset{1}{2},\overset{1}{7}44 \\
\hline
1,929
\end{array}
\qquad
\begin{array}{r}
8,\overset{1}{3}5\overset{1}{4} \\
- 5,\overset{1}{7}\overset{1}{3}9 \\
\hline
2,615
\end{array}
\qquad
\begin{array}{r}
8,\overset{1}{0}\overset{1}{0}\overset{1}{0} \\
- \overset{1}{5},\overset{1}{2}78 \\
\hline
2,722
\end{array}
$$

Beginning Multiplication and Division

You will find that it is much easier to teach 2-place multiplication and long division if you use graph paper. **Note:** For those who really need help, try to find workbooks called SLAM multiplication and/or SLAM division. They have a very logical, step-by-step approach for the child who is having real difficulty.

Star Math

Students love this method in which a "star" is used to mark places while they are multiplying. In reality, use an asterisk (*) instead of a star, however, or you will be spending your time teaching students how to draw stars instead of computing. Also, have students cross out a digit once it has been used to multiply.

Casting Out Nines

Children love tricks for doing school work and casting out nines is no exception. Teach it to children as a checking method. To do the basic method, look within a given number for two digits that, when combined, total nine. Cross these numbers out and then add the remaining numbers. If this total has a two digit answer, add the digits together. Continue until a one digit answer remains.

> ### Example
>
> $3, (1\cdot5) \, 6 \longrightarrow 1 + 5 = 6$

Math *(cont.)*

Checking Addition Using Casting Out Nines

Add the digits you get in the addends from casting out nines, and they will match the cast out sum.

Added up, these make:

$$2,256 = 2+5= \qquad 7$$
$$+ 5,732 = 3+5= \qquad +8$$
$$\overline{8,088} = 2+4=⑥ \quad 1+5=⑥$$

Checking Subtraction Using Casting Out Nines

Subtract. Cast out nines. The subtrahend added to the difference should match the minuend. (Remember that addition and subtraction are opposites.)

$$6,837 = 15 = ⑥$$
$$- 5,725 = 10 = 1$$
$$\overline{1,112} = 5 \qquad 5 + 1 = ⑥$$

Note: It is also of value to teach them how to add up from the difference to check their work, but **do not** do it at the same time. Looking at the example above, start with the 2 in the difference, add it to the 5 above = 7, then 1+2=3, 1+7=8, 1+5=6. (Sometimes it is necessary to "carry.")

Checking Multiplication Using Casting Out Nines

Cast out the nines and then add up the digits in the multiplicands and the product. Multiply the multiplicands, add up the digits again, and if this number matches the sum of the product, the answer is (probably) right.

$$
\begin{array}{ll}
256 & = 1\ 3 = 4 \\
\underline{\text{x } 43} & \quad \underline{\text{x } 7} \\
768 & \qquad 28=10=1 \\
10,240 & \\
\overline{11,008} & = 10 = 1
\end{array}
$$

$$
\begin{array}{ll}
742 & = \qquad 4 \\
\underline{\text{x } 671} & =14 = \underline{\text{x } 5} \\
742 & \qquad 20 = 2 \\
51,940 & \\
\underline{+ 445,200} & \\
\overline{497,882} & = 20 = 2
\end{array}
$$

Math *(cont.)*

Checking Division Using Casting Out Nines

Casting out nines is done by making the quotient and divisor a single digit and then multiplying them. Next, add the remainder and again get a single digit. Compare this with the dividend as a single digit, and, if they are the same, then the answer is (probably) right.

Example:

$$42\overline{)3{,}589} \quad 85 \text{ R19}$$

$$8 + 5 = 13 = 4$$
$$4 + 2 = 6 \qquad \Big] \quad \textbf{Step 1}$$
$$4 \times 6 = 24 = 6 \qquad] \quad \textbf{Step 2}$$
$$6 + 19 = 25 = \textcircled{7} \qquad] \quad \textbf{Step 3}$$
$$3 + 5 + 8 + \cancel{9} = 16 = \textcircled{7} \qquad] \quad \textbf{Step 4}$$

Steps for Checking Division

1. Cast out nines in quotient and divisor.
2. Multiply answers in step 1.
3. Add remainder to answer in step 2 and cast out nines.
4. Find sum of digits in dividend. Cast out nines. Make answer a single digit and compare it to answer in step 3.

Card Games

A deck of cards is a great tool for teaching math facts and concepts. Check your closest warehouse store for inexpensive decks. If you can, pick up extras to put in the children's disaster kits or keep several decks at a math center.

Teach the students card games for the skills you are working on. Many students will know none or only a few games. (Cards are another example of a manipulative where you must explain the use, firmly saying that no poker or gambling will be allowed and that any students who do become involved in such will no longer participate in any card games at school.) In addition to books on card games available in the library, try the game on page 77.

Math *(cont.)*

Card Games *(cont.)*

Ninety-nine

Players: 3–6

Materials: one deck of cards, three dealt to each player, the rest face down in a pile; card values written on the board or on cards for each group

Object: Do not go over 99, or you lose.

The first player places one card face up in the center, announcing the card's value and then takes a new card from the deck. The next player chooses a card, places it on top of the first, announces the combined value of the two cards, and then draws a new card. Play continues in this manner until a player is unable to play without the total sum going over 99. That player is out of the game. The top card reverts to its face value (see exceptions below) and play continues until all players are eliminated except the winner.

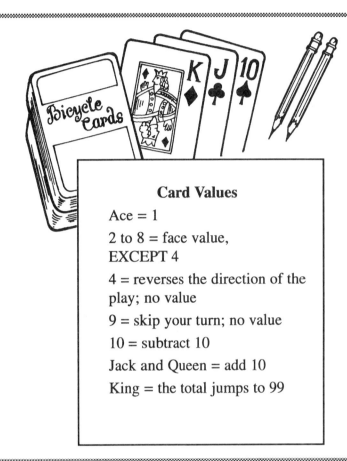

Card Values

Ace = 1

2 to 8 = face value, EXCEPT 4

4 = reverses the direction of the play; no value

9 = skip your turn; no value

10 = subtract 10

Jack and Queen = add 10

King = the total jumps to 99

Fractions

Vocabulary: A trick for remembering the denominator is that it is down; both words begin with "D." The word "denominator" tells how many parts into which the whole was divided; the numerator tells the number of parts selected for a particular purpose.

Understanding Fractions: Children tend to think that the larger the denominator, the larger the amount. Have the children make their own fraction circles. Run off whole circles and circles divided into halves, quarters, thirds, fifths, sixths, and eighths on multicolored paper so they can see and feel the difference. They can keep the circle fractions in large envelopes and pull them out for reference.

Rules of Divisibility: Recognizing which numbers can be divided by which will be easier if you review (or teach) children that even numbers are always divisible by 2. Numbers divisible by three are easy to recognize: add up the digits within a number. If the sum is divisible by three, then so is the original number. For instance, the digits in 135 add up to 9; 9 is divisible by 3 and, therefore, so is 135. Finally, show them how easy it is to tell if a number is divisible by 5 by seeing if it ends with 0 or 5. Now, you're ready to do fraction trees.

Math *(cont.)*

Graphing

A continual problem children have with graphing is remembering which direction to graph the first number in a pair—up or across? Alphabetical order works well as a memory device for both across and up for positive numbers, and across and down for negative numbers. Also, they can remember to plot the *x* axis before the *y* axis because *x* comes before *y* in the alphabet. One final way is to have children think about an elevator—they must walk across to the elevator and then ride it either up or down.

Five in a Row: After drawing and teaching about graphs on the board a few times, divide the class into two teams. Have them take turns, going from one group to another, with each person getting a chance to call out five coordinates which you plot on the board, placing either an *x* or an *o* on the grid. Once the team gets five *x*'s or *o*'s in a row, that team wins a point.

When the whole class understands the game, then give them their own grid paper so they can figure out the numbers before they place their *x*'s or *o*'s. Soon they'll understand how to place coordinates and won't need the grid paper to help them play the game.

Greater Than, Less Than

The signs of < or > can be very hard for students to understand. Instead of trying to get students to memorize what they stand for, have them think of a hungry alligator. The hungry alligator is going to eat the biggest thing, not waste time on little stuff. Thus, the mouth is open to the largest "food," or number.

Math *(cont.)*

Learning New Terms

A chart displayed in a prominent place in the classroom can provide students with a valuable resource for new math terms or concepts.

Math Glossary	
42 addend + 26 addend 68 sum	42 minuend - 36 subtrahend 6 difference
9 multiplicand x 6 multiplicand 54 product	6 ←quotient 9)54 ←dividend ↑ divisor

Logic and Fun Math Games

On pages 80–87 are reproducible math games. "Five-in-a-Row" and "Box It!" may both be played on regular graph paper in place of the work sheet. Many of the other games can be played on regular paper once the students have used the work sheets to learn them.

Note: Students may have been taught by parents or other teachers a different way of doing math than the way you know. Please invite them to share their methods with you. Some of the ways of doing math may be worth sharing with the whole class. You may want to allow students to use any method they wish as long as they can show you how they arrive at a correct answer.

Use page 87 as a bulletin board idea, especially for Open House. Have students make large numbers on the bulletin board paper and complete page 87 for the bulletin board in their free time. Or have the children complete it for the hundredth day of the school year. You could also put the ditto in the file folder for your substitute to use.

Math *(cont.)*

Box It!

Directions: Find a partner and a pencil to play this game Take turns drawing a single horizontal or vertical line from one dot to another. When you complete a box, put your initials inside it and draw another line. The person who makes the most boxes is the winner.

Math *(cont.)*

Five-in-a-Row

Directions: Use these grids to plan a strategy for a whole-class game.
Teacher: See page 78.

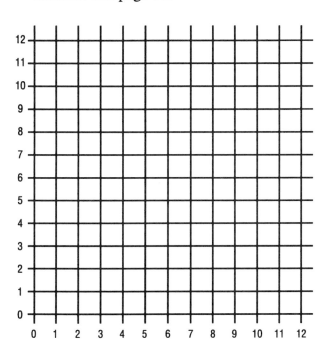

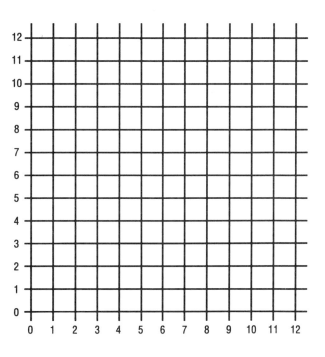

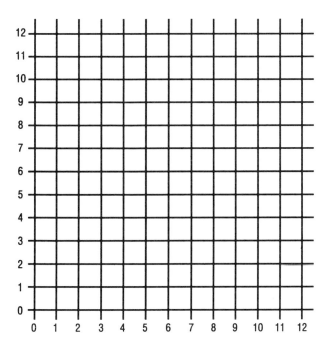

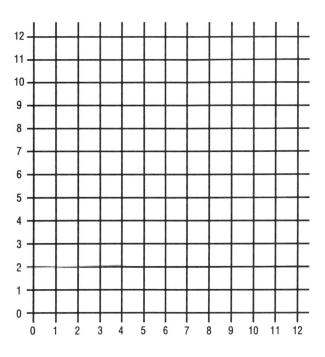

Math *(cont.)*

Logic Puzzles

Directions: Cut out these four pieces and put them together to make each of the following:

- a square
- a parallelogram
- a square with a gap in the middle

Math *(cont.)*

Nim

Directions: Take away 1, 2, or 3 cubes. The player who takes away the last cube wins. Play a few games and try to find the winning strategy.

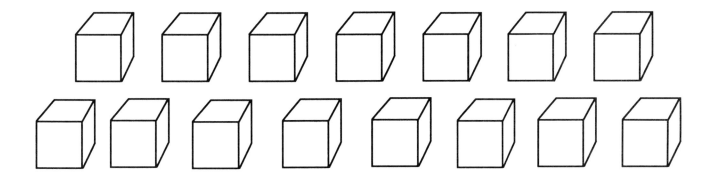

Nim

Directions: Take away 1, 2, or 3 cubes. The player who takes away the last cube wins. Play a few games and try to find the winning strategy.

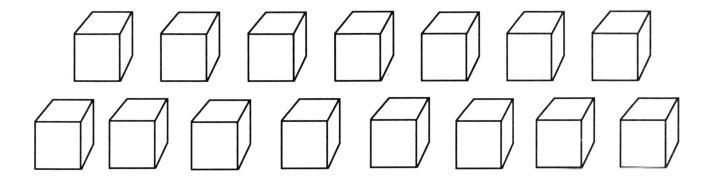

Math *(cont.)*

Nim II

Directions: Take turns taking away 1, 2, or 3 cubes from any row. The player to remove the last cube loses the game.

Math *(cont.)*

Puzzle Shapes

Directions: Cut these puzzles out and see how fast you can solve them.

Squared Away

Use these pieces to make a square.

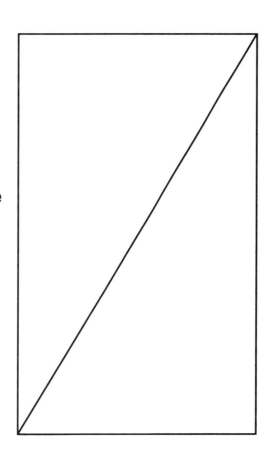

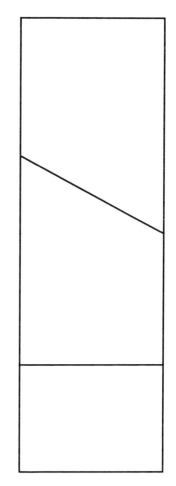

The Great "T" Puzzle

Use these pieces to make a capital "T."

Math *(cont.)*

Sprout

Directions: Draw a "sprout"—a line—from one circle to another. After you have drawn a sprout, draw a circle on that line. Now it is your partner's turn to draw a sprout from one circle to another. Keep playing this way until one of you can no longer draw a sprout. The last person able to make a play is the winner.

Rules

1. You may not cross any lines.

2. A circle may have only three sprouts coming from it. After three sprouts, the circle is filled in and that circle may no longer be used.

When this paper is finished, get blank paper and make your own circles. Try beginning with three, four or five circles. Can you come up with a strategy for winning?

Game One	Game Two

Game Three	Game Four

 Math *(cont.)*

Number Magic

Directions: Use the numbers 1, 2, 3, 4, and 5 to make math problems expressing the numbers from 1 to 100. You may use the numbers 1 through 5 only once in each problem, but you may also use any math functions you wish. For example, the number 19 can be expressed as 23–4 or as [2 x (5 + 4)]+1.

1= _____	34= _____	67= _____
2= _____	35= _____	68= _____
3= _____	36= _____	69= _____
4= _____	37= _____	70= _____
5= _____	38= _____	71= _____
6= _____	39= _____	72= _____
7= _____	40= _____	73= _____
8= _____	41= _____	74= _____
9= _____	42= _____	75= _____
10= _____	43= _____	76= _____
11= _____	44= _____	77= _____
12= _____	45= _____	78= _____
13= _____	46= _____	79= _____
14= _____	47= _____	80= _____
15= _____	48= _____	81= _____
16= _____	49= _____	82= _____
17= _____	50= _____	83= _____
18= _____	51= _____	84= _____
19= _____	52= _____	85= _____
20= _____	53= _____	86= _____
21= _____	54= _____	87= _____
22= _____	55= _____	88= _____
23= _____	56= _____	89= _____
24= _____	57= _____	90= _____
25= _____	58= _____	91= _____
26= _____	59= _____	92= _____
27= _____	60= _____	93= _____
28= _____	61= _____	94= _____
29= _____	62= _____	95= _____
30= _____	63= _____	96= _____
31= _____	64= _____	97= _____
32= _____	65= _____	98= _____
33= _____	66= _____	99= _____

100= _____

Monitors

Keep a list of monitors in the back of your plan book and mark off each job as a student is assigned to it. Change your monitors weekly so that each student has had a chance to do every job at least once during the school year. List the jobs on laminated tagboard and then write in the students' names in water soluble pen.

Suggested Monitors and Their Jobs

Office: Deliver materials and notes to the office and to other teachers.

Door: Get the key to unlock the door after breaks and lock it when you leave the room. Also makes sure it's locked and the room is empty for emergency drills and any needed signs are hung on the door.

Pencil: Make sure pencils in the pencil can on the teacher's desk are sharp and sharpen new ones. (See "Pencils," page 90.)

Paper: Pass out papers. Warn the teacher when paper supply is getting low.

Ball: Makes sure the balls are firm, that they have a legible room number on them, and that the students who take them out to recess bring them back. **Note**: Tell ball monitors to allow any student only one turn a day taking out equipment because of the tendency to favor friends.

Flag: Lead the class in the flag salute. (Have the students say the pledge right after they come in and take their chairs down from their desks since they're already standing. It also keeps those who refrain from saying the pledge comfortable.)

Book: Keep classroom books straightened and stamp the library books when going to the library.

Board: Change the date on the chalkboard every morning and on the calendar. (Erase the board after every subject—if the teacher is finished with the work—and clean the chalk ledge.)

Line Leaders: Demonstrate to others how to behave. The quietest line goes in the room first, goes to lunch first, etc.

Pets: Change the pet's water and check the food supply daily. Clean the cage weekly, although a snake's home can go for a month without cleaning.

Sink: Clean the sink and counter area.

O

Oral Reading

Please read aloud to your students every day. They need to develop their listening skills and to use their imaginations. Many of them also need to be introduced to books, never having had anyone read aloud to them.

Put a lot of expression in your voice; even dress up in parts or bring props to class to introduce the book or to highlight parts of it. For longer books, try to stop in an interesting place so they will look forward to hearing more tomorrow. Before you begin reading the next day, ask a child to review what has already happened in the book.

Fairy tales are a very good choice for kindergarten and first grades, and there are many good collections. Few children are read to in this television age, and many do not know even simple tales like "Goldilocks and the Three Bears." For second grade, depending on the sophistication of your students, you might try simple chapter books. Most children enjoy books by Roald Dahl. Dahl's *James and the Giant Peach* is a good selection for grades two to five, *George's Marvelous Medicine* for grades three to six, and *The BFG* for grades four to six. Of course, there are many other good read-aloud books; talk to your school librarian or local bookseller for ideas.

Other Teachers

Please ask other teachers for help. Most teachers are in the profession because they want to help others and will be delighted that you came to them for advice.

Other teachers can be a good resource for help handling tough discipline problems, conducting difficult parent conferences, teaching tough math concepts—in short, anything you can think of. If you are a beginning teacher, your district may have a mentor program in which an expert teacher is assigned to guide you. If not, try to find those with a teaching style that you would like to emulate and then find out how they do it. You may even be able to observe your chosen expert; ask your principal if this is a possibility.

P

Parent Conferences

First, do not wait until parent conferences to communicate with parents. Parents are your most important ally, so send home letters about what is going on in your classroom, little notes of praise, or art projects that are sure parent pleasers before conferences are scheduled.

When it comes time for conferences, remember that you are communicating with parents whose children are the most important thing in the world. Be diplomatic and kind. A good rule of thumb is to deliver positive messages about each student first and then state any areas which need improvement. For each such area, have a prescription ready, such as establishing a time and place to do homework for a student who has trouble completing it.

Once you have established a relationship with the parents, you can ask for their help. For example, when a student has trouble completing work, have the student and parent sign and return a work contract and then send home a daily report (pages 134 and 135). Again, be sure to note any positive signs in the student's behavior in order to continue a good relationship between yourself and the parents as well as the student.

Paper Distribution and Collection

The very first time you need to distribute or collect materials, demonstrate and talk the students through the procedure you wish them to follow. If items need to be collected in alphabetical order, collect them during roll call to save time recording grades or checking off forms.

Otherwise, collect materials by having the student at the back of each row pass his or her paper forward to the next student, who then passes both papers to the third student, and so on. When the students in the front of each row receive the materials, they can pass them to the center of the room.

If the students are sitting in groups, assign a leader to each group to whom students will pass materials. The leaders can then bring the materials to you or place them in a collection box (plastic dishwashing tubs work well).

Pencils

Simple though they are, managing pencils can be a problem. Begin by providing each student with two sharpened pencils. When they need a new pencil, tell them they must trade in their old one. Pencils can either be sharpened by a designated monitor or by students at a certain time every day—perhaps before beginning a math lesson. Some students seem to lose pencils like a flower loses petals; deal with them individually. If it is permissible, have those students bring in their own supply. If not, try allowing the students some special privilege, such as a few extra minutes with the class pet, if they go an entire week without asking for a new pencil.

IF YOU TAKE 1, bring 1 BACK NEXT TIME

P

Posters

Laminate posters if you can. Usually, this is something your district can do for you. If you can't get them laminated, put masking tape around the back edges, or at least on the corners. That way the edges won't tear when the posters are taken down.

If you are making your own posters, add pictures from an educational supply store before you laminate.

Door Posters: "If you do not know, do not leave!" This discourages students from saying they didn't understand an assignment as an excuse for not completing an assignment. Tell them when you are available to help or insist that they call a study buddy.

Wall Posters: A poster with the following information provides students with productive activities during those times when all of their assigned work has been completed.

Free Time?

☐ 1. Read a book.

☐ 2. Complete work from another subject.

☐ 3. Study for an upcoming test.

☐ 4. Straighten the books in the classroom library.

☐ 5. Scrub the sink and counter.

☐ 6. Play with a classroom pet.

☐ 7. Get scratch paper and draw.

☐ 8. Straighten your desk.

☐ 9. Help someone.

☐ 10. Ask your teacher if he or she needs help.

☐ 11. Pass out corrected work.

☐ 12. Straighten the paper drawer and/or the construction paper.

Another idea is to put up a poster with quotes from famous (or not so famous) people. You can discuss or have the students write about them as a filler. Look in *Bartlett's Familiar Quotations* and keep your eyes open for new ones to add to a list in your plan book.

You may also want to keep a copy of your classroom rules posted at all times.

P

Posters *(cont.)*

Calendars as Posters: There are many calendars on the market with great photos of art, animals, places to travel, the Old West, etc. You can often buy them in February or March at a greatly reduced price. They are also an inexpensive source for pictures related to social studies, seasons, etc.

If you teach a primary grade, it's nice to send home a monthly calendar with school functions, holidays, and maybe even homework assignments listed on it. Create a blank calendar with five rows of seven squares and then add the name of the month, the days, and any noteworthy functions or holidays. Children can then glue the calendar onto the bottom half of a sheet of construction paper and add an appropriate drawing on the top half.

Making Neat Posters: You can letter posters neatly if you put a piece of lined tagboard on top of your poster board, lining up the bottom edge of the poster board with the lines at the bottom of the tagboard. Use the top of the tagboard as a straight edge and write with a marker to just above the edge of the tagboard. When one line of writing is finished, pull the tagboard down as many spaces as you want your lettering to be large and continue writing. In this way you have created evenly spaced lines easily and without lines drawn on the poster board.

Storing Posters and Cutouts: Cut plain tagboard into lengthwise strips and glue them to two whole pieces of tagboard to make a folder. Make one for each subject area to stay organized.

Practice Theory

Practice is what helps us retain new material. Practice needs to match the objective of the lesson. These are some guidelines that help to make practice more effective. When learning something new, the practice period needs to be short, intense, and on the smallest amount of the material that still retains meaning. For example, if students are assigned to memorize a poem, learning only one line at a time might lose the meaning of the poem. Working on a stanza and then taking a break will result in learning the poem more efficiently.

P

Practice Theory *(cont.)*

After learning something new, maintenance is required by reviewing over time. For example, in the case of the poem, students might review the poem after two days to see if they still know it. If they do, they can check again after four to five days. If they forget, they will need to go back and practice it until they know it again. Keep this in mind as you assign classwork or homework. In addition, when students must practice material with many items of the same type, such as math, consider whether they need 50 examples when they could successfully and accurately complete 20 and still have received adequate practice. By choosing fewer examples to accomplish the same goal, you decrease the time you will need to correct work and avoid student frustration over having to complete the additional "busy" work.

Encourage practice at home as a method of retaining new material. Remind parents and students that although specific class assignments may not be given every night, students are expected to practice or review some of the new materials they learned in school. This, like reading for a period of time at home each night, is an important skill for all students. Finally, research shows that the brain processes memory as we sleep, so advise students to get a good rest each night.

Use the general form below as part of your homework assignment routine or adapt one that more specifically meets your needs.

Date: _____

Homework Practice

_____
Student's Name

practiced his/her

_____ **at home.**

_____
Parent's Signature

Record Keeping

You need to decide what written records will indicate how students are learning. There are many places during the implementation of a lesson at which you can observe student progress. You will need to devise a method of recording observations. A clipboard with an attached pen provides a handy holder for a record sheet which can be carried to wherever instruction is occurring. You may wish to duplicate the form on page 95 and add a few blank pieces of paper on which to record specific anecdotal comments.

Although most districts provide teachers with a grade book, you may find that forms like the one on page 96 are easily adapted for specific record-keeping needs.

R

Record Keeping (cont.)

Observation Sheet

Lesson Step	Purpose	Observations	Student Names
Set	Get students ready to learn.	Is anyone not ready to learn this material?	
Instruction	Teach the lesson.	Who has attention and/or comprehension problems?	
Guided Practice	Practice new learning.	Who is experiencing difficulty applying the concepts taught?	
Closure	Solidify connections between learning and practice.	Who needs re-teaching?	
Independent Practice	Practice without the teacher.	Who is/is not performing well independently?	
Mastery Check	Test (may cover at the end of several lessons).	Who has/has not mastered the concepts?	

Notes/Comments: _____

© Teacher Created Materials, Inc.   95   #029 The Busy Teacher's Survival Guide

Registers

Keep in your register a list of how to mark absences and what constitutes an excused, unexcused or personal necessity absence. Also keep your district's calendar for the year and a flat 6" ruler in a holder taped inside the cover to use for lining out holidays and short enrollment for students.

Registers are not much fun, but they do get easier with practice. Get another teacher to show you how to do it—unless your secretary does it or your district does it on a computer. Registers are due at the end of every school month, and in most districts you will need to keep every tardy and absence note, so be forewarned. Sometimes absence excuses are difficult for students to remember, so reward the students with a raffle ticket if they bring in an excuse the day they return. This takes less time than calling parents to verify absences.

Report Cards

Report cards are time consuming; consider investing in a grade calculator, usually available at an educational supply store. Grade calculators will save you hours of time for relatively little money.

As for the actual report cards—try to get extras. You will always make at least one mistake and need to do the report card over.

Do the best you can to be positive but also be honest. This is a chance for parents to help their children. Give specific ways for the student to improve.

Have the students' cumulative records with you on final conference day so that you can work on them between conferences. As you write comments, be aware that the records are open for parents to see, so phrase things very carefully—for instance, "Needs encouragement" instead of "Lazy."

R

Record Keeping *(cont.)*

Observation Sheet

Lesson Step	Purpose	Observations	Student Names
Set	Get students ready to learn.	Is anyone not ready to learn this material?	
Instruction	Teach the lesson.	Who has attention and/or comprehension problems?	
Guided Practice	Practice new learning.	Who is experiencing difficulty applying the concepts taught?	
Closure	Solidify connections between learning and practice.	Who needs reteaching?	
Independent Practice	Practice without the teacher.	Who is/is not performing well independently?	
Mastery Check	Test (may occur at the end of several lessons).	Who has/has not mastered the concepts?	

Notes/Comments: _____

_____

_____

_____

_____

_____

R

Record Sheet for Assignments

✓ Assignment is complete and turned in on time.

◯ Assignment is missing, or the student is absent.   ✓ Assignment is turned in late.

Student Names												
1.												
2.												
3.												
4.												
5.												
6.												
7.												
8.												
9.												
10.												
11.												
12.												
13.												
14.												
15.												
16.												
17.												
18.												
19.												
20.												
21.												
22.												
23.												
24.												
25.												
26.												
27.												
28.												
29.												
30.												

R

Resources

Besides the teacher next door, try these resources:

Stan Adair
2936 E. Pico
Fresno, CA 93726
This company provides great math flash cards!

Argus
Call (800) 527-4748 for a free brochure on their posters, banners, and certificates.

Calculated Industries, Inc.
22720 Savi Ranch Parkway
Yorba Linda, CA 92686
This is an excellent resource for time-saving calculators for teachers.

Marcy Cook
33112 Diamond Avenue
Balboa Island, CA 92662
Marcy Cook is a math consultant who publishes her own materials.

Creative Publications
These are good resources for math teaching materials.

Dale Seymour Publications
(800) 872-1100
Excellent math and science resources are provided.

Great Explorations in Math and Science (GEMS)
Lawrence Hall of Science
University of CA at Berkeley
Berkeley, CA 94720
(510) 642-7771
This is a great source for sciences and math projects which are interactive and expand into language arts. Write for a catalog.

Instructor Magazine
555 Broadway
New York, NY 10012-3999

McDougal, Littell & Company
(800) 225-3809
This company publishes the *Daily Oral Language Plus* booklet, which is great for teaching ESL.

Oriental Trading Company
(800) 228-2269
This company carries inexpensive prizes and holiday decorations.

Plastics Manufacturing Company
P.O. Box 769045
Dallas, TX 75376-9045
Write to this company for ideas for making your own plate projects.

Teacher Created Materials, Inc.
For a catalog, call (800) 662-4321 or fax (800) 525-1254.
This company is an excellent resource for classroom tested materials.

Tricks of the Trade with Cards by Chuck Lund
Activity Resources Company, Inc.
P.O. Box 4875
Hayward, CA 94540

325 Creative Prompts For Personal Journals by J. A. Senn
Scholastic, Inc.
P.O. Box 120
Bergenfield, NJ 07621
Orders: 800-325-6149
This book provides lots of good ideas for daily journals.

Seating Charts

Seating charts are helpful in a variety of situations. They are invaluable to substitutes. Create a seating chart after the first few weeks of school. Special seating charts can be made for use with cooperative learning groups to be sure that your students work together in the best possible learning environment.

Choose from among the seating plans presented below and on pages 99-103.

Teacher

Seating Charts *(cont.)*

Teacher

Seating Charts *(cont.)*

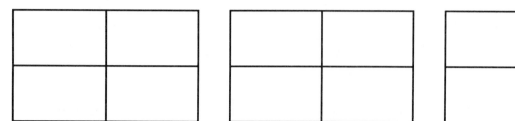

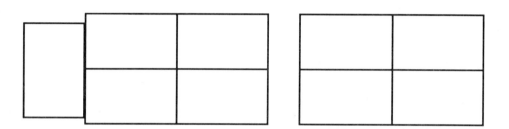

Teacher

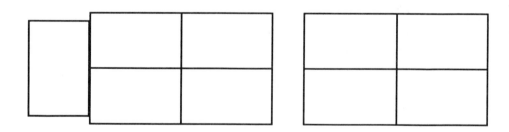

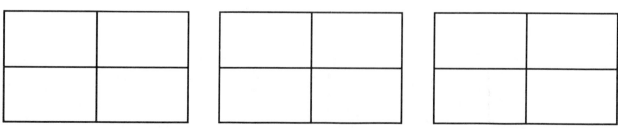

Seating Charts *(cont.)*

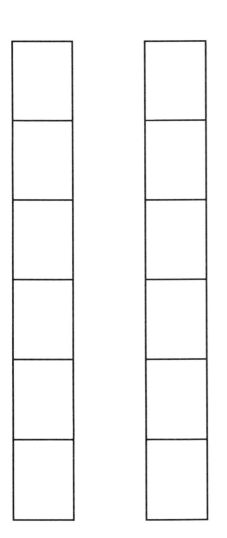
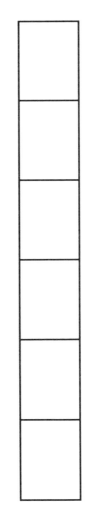
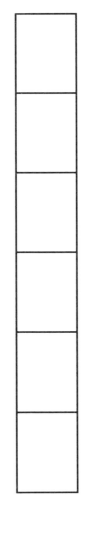

Teacher

Seating Charts *(cont.)*

Teacher

Seating Charts *(cont.)*

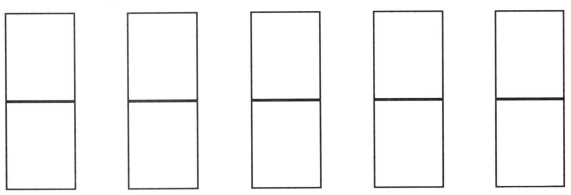

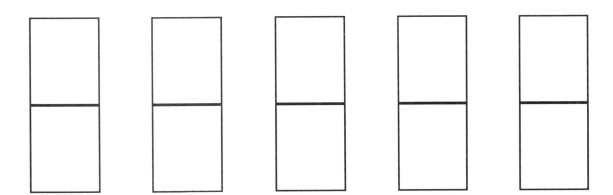

Teacher

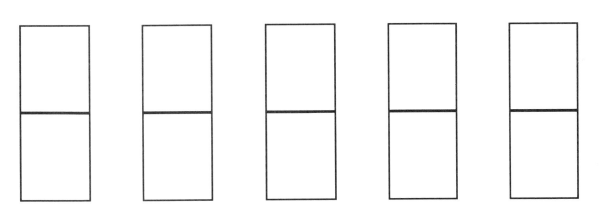

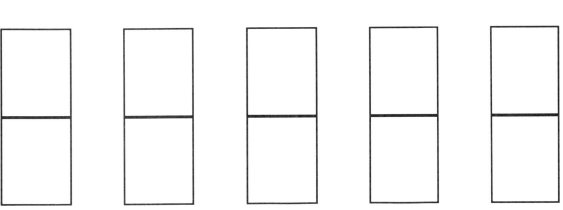

S

Speeches

Have students give speeches once a week. Their speeches can be oral book reports, deal with history or science, or poems they choose to memorize. The speeches can also be on other general topics; the following is a list that you may wish to copy and keep in your lesson plan book.

Speech Ideas

- Tell a joke (not a riddle)
- Show and tell how something works
- Show and tell about an item from early childhood
- Your most embarrassing moment
- A Holiday Gift
- What I Would Like to Learn
- A Special Person in My Life
- An Unusual Animal (research project)
- An Unusual Animal as a Pet (research project, with pros and cons of ownership)
- A Famous Woman
- A Famous Man
- My Favorite Place
- Someone I'd Like to Meet
- The Worst Experience of My Life
- My Trip
- My Favorite Book
- Things I Dislike at School and Ways to Fix Them
- The Best Thing That Ever Happened to Me
- Tell a story
- Memorize a poem
- "Sell" a CD
- Memorize the "Gettysburg Address"
- Where to Take a Vacation (research project)
- My Best Friend
- When I'm a Parent
- When Someone Dies
- Travelling Back Through Time
- My favorite poem, story, saying, speech, etc.

S

Speeches *(cont.)*

Speech Evaluation Form

Speech by: _____ The grade you earned:_____

Would you like to do better? Next time, work on the things which have a check, and you can—you will!

You need to improve in the following areas:

Make your speech longer   _____

Bring required material   _____

Your speech needs to be more:

interesting   _____

organized   _____

informative   _____

detailed, with good examples given   _____

You need to make your voice:

louder   _____

softer   _____

faster   _____

slower   _____

clearer   _____

more varied, with better expression   _____

You need to:

stand straighter   _____

be more relaxed   _____

use more hand gestures   _____

look at everyone   _____

spend more time practicing
your speech at home   _____

Spelling

Keep a colored file folder for vocabulary on your desk with blank paper in it. When you run across misspellings in students' work or vocabulary words you want to teach from social studies, reading, etc., write them down. Also keep a list of the top 100 most misspelled words. Get these from your resource teacher. Keep a master list in your file and cross out words on your copy as you use them during the year. With these combined lists, you will have more than enough spelling words to last the year.

On Mondays, give the children a spelling quiz. This way students will truly know which words they need help on and can take the list home and study. They need to study not only the spelling but also the meaning; on spelling tests, try giving students the definitions and have them write down and spell the words.

For that first quiz, have students write their spelling words on the left side of the paper. After the quiz, say and spell the words. Students can touch each letter as you say it, circling the letter or letters they miss. Next, carefully write the word on the board and give them hints to remember how each word is spelled. When their list is complete, check their papers later in the day. If a child makes a mistake copying the new word, have him or her copy that word or words ten times for homework.

Assign spelling activities on Tuesdays and Wednesdays (see pages 107-108). On Thursdays, give a pretest: say the word, use it in a sentence, and say the word again. Use a few words at the beginning of the sentence so that the students must capitalize them. For another few words, give the definition instead. The last three words are always in sentences, and most students should try to write the whole sentence. You can use these sentences to help children learn whatever you are working on in class, such as quotation marks.

After the Thursday pretest, students put their pencils in their desks while you write the correct answers on the board, listing only those words which you have defined or which need capital letters, plus the dictated sentences. Students check their own papers with crayons or colored pencils, using a check mark after the incorrect word or sentence. Check their papers; any misspelled word must be copied 10 times and whole sentences copied five times.

Thursday's pretest should be taken home, the assigned work should be completed, and the parents should sign the pretest. The signature allows the parent to be aware of how the child is doing; they can offer help, if desired.

Some students are poor spellers; assign only as much of the list as you think they can handle. Do not be afraid to give them more if they get to be good spellers or to make their list smaller if you need to.

S

Spelling *(cont.)*

Spelling Activities

❏ Configuration Puzzle

Students will mix up the order of their spelling words and then make boxes around the imaginary letter of each word. They are not to put the letters in the boxes because the next day they will give their puzzle to someone else to do.

❏ Definitions

Have students look up their spelling words in the dictionary and then copy the part of speech and the definition that makes the most sense to them. Allow them to copy the sentence in the dictionary as long as they have the definition; make them responsible for demonstrating that they know the meaning of each word.

❏ Sentences

Students can write original sentences in which the meaning of each vocabulary word is clear. Have them underline each word they used from the list. After each sentence, have them leave four lines blank. When they turn their papers, correct the sentences on the line right below theirs; then, they must write each incorrect sentence two times.

❏ Handwriting

If many students in your class have poor handwriting, have them write each spelling word five times each in their best handwriting. They should have their copy of the words you wrote so carefully on the board for them on Monday, so their letters should be formed correctly. If an upper grade student has really poor handwriting, have him or her practice on primary or third grade handwriting paper. (If you do not know which paper is which, have an experienced teacher show you.) You can combine this activity with putting the words in alphabetical order.

❏ Story Writing

Have students use their spelling words in a story. You decide how many words they are to use; the number may vary according to individual student ability.

❏ Illustrations

Draw a picture representing five of the spelling words. (This can be much harder than it sounds; check over your list before you give this assignment.)

❏ Syllables

Have students look up the words in the dictionary and copy the syllable breaks. You can then have them categorize the words by the number of syllables and then alphabetize them.

❏ Word Sentences

Use as many words from the vocabulary list as you can to make sentences with each letter in the word forming the first letter of a word in the sentence. For example, the word "paint" could be used as a base for writing "Paula ate ice cream nine times." You may wish to let them work with partners at first if they have difficulty with this assignment.

Spelling *(cont.)*

Spelling Activities *(cont.)*

❏ Small Words

Students are to find the small words in their spelling words. Making it into a contest is the most fun, and many reluctant students will amaze you with all the words they can find. (If it is an unusual word, they must copy down the meaning.) Use the following rules:

- Use no foreign words or proper nouns.

- Words must be two or more letters.

- Each word counts as one point.

- If a student uses a nonexistent word, two points are taken off.

- The person with the most points wins.

❏ Word Search

Have students put the words into boxes on graph paper. The spelling words go in first, written horizontally, vertically, or diagonally. Random letters fill in all other spaces. The list of spelling words must be written below the grid. The next day, students exchange papers with partners and words are circled as they are found, as well as crossed out in the list below.

❏ Vowels

Teach the students the following rule: "When two vowels go walking, the first does the talking." Now they will know that when they hear a long vowel, they usually need to look for a second vowel following it.

❏ Crossword Puzzle

This activity will take a lot of effort on your part the first few times the students do it, especially getting the students to understand that the numbers move across the paper, then down, like a typewriter, but for competent students this is a good one. Give students two sheets of graph paper. On the first sheet—the master—they fill in the letters for their puzzle. They then draw heavy lines around the outside of each word. Next, they lay the second piece of graph paper over the master sheet and copy over the lines around the word, using a ruler. Then, they put the numbers on the top sheet and write the definitions below the puzzle. The next day, they may exchange papers with a partner who gives a grade for both definitions and neatness.

❏ Synonyms, Antonyms, and Homonyms

Write spelling words in a list on the left side of the paper and draw three additional columns with "Synonyms," "Homonyms," and "Antonyms" written across the top. At least one category must be filled in for each spelling word.

S

Spelling *(cont.)*

Word Search Form

Directions: Create a word search using your spelling words. Begin by penciling in your spelling words on the grid below. The tricky part is to make sure that words "cross" in an appropriate place; for example, the "a" in "cat" needs to cross the "a" in "hat."

You can earn two grades from a partner for this word search—one for neatness, spelling, using all the words and crossing the words appropriately, and another grade for the difficulty of your puzzle. Words can go in any of eight directions:

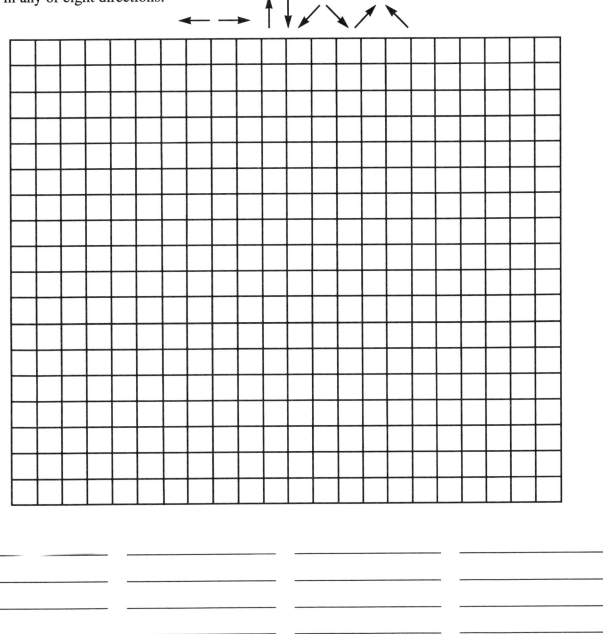

S

Starting Off the Year

First, find someone who can help you! Perhaps a willing teacher or the school secretary can tell you where supplies are and how to get them. Do you have a budget? Do you need to fill in forms to get supplies? Are there forms to send home with the students on the first day? Where are the textbooks and how can you get them? Are there any students available to help?

The beginning of the school year is an extraordinarily busy time. The following list is meant to give you a realistic guideline of what needs to be accomplished before the children arrive on the first day. The list can help you group your errands, trips to the copier, and so forth, so that you do not end up feeling like a squirrel running here, there, and everywhere, trying to get ready. You may wish to star the items you need or must do; check everything off as it gets done.

Student Supplies

Unless your district requires students to bring their own materials, be prepared to supply each of them with the following:

- crayons
- pencils appropriate for grade level (Ask.)
- erasers
- glue or glue sticks
- rulers
- scissors (Get containers for these.)
- textbooks (Get two to three extra.)
- writing paper appropriate for grade level (Ask.)
- extras: pens, pencil top erasers

Teacher Supplies

- construction paper (Get three reams of white plus multicolors; think holidays.)
- correction fluid
- envelopes (legal size)
- file cards (Cut them in half for name tags; use them whole for flash cards.)
- file folders (Buy a box at a warehouse store.)
- lesson plan book (See pages 54–55.)
- lists of school rules, telephone numbers, map of the school, teachers' names, etc. (Ask the school secretary.)
- marking pens—large permanent ones for posters and marking room number on balls, plus colored ones for correcting papers, etc.
- masking tape, wide and narrow
- paper clips, large and small
- ink pens, various colors
- register (See page 94.)
- rubber bands, all sizes
- safety pins, large and small
- transparent tape
- stapler (three or more)
- staple remover
- staples
- straight pins
- tagboard, lined and unlined
- whistle

Starting Off the Year *(cont.)*

Teacher Supplies*(cont.)*

- address labels with your name and school and school address
- bean bags (Make them.)
- brads
- colored chalk
- cones for PE
- E-Z Grader (Buy one from an educational supply store.)
- E-Z stamp (See above.)
- overhead projector pens
- paper cutter
- paper punches, with and without designs
- raffle tickets
- sticky notes

- sink supplies: antibacterial soap and hand lotion
- stamp with your name
- T pins
- Tacky Fingers (Buy them from a stationery store. They help with sorting papers.)
- thimble (Use it to push pins into the bulletin board.)
- three-hole punch (Get one that will go inside your binder.)
- tools (hammer, thin nails, pliers, screwdrivers—both flathead and Phillips)
- yardstick or metric stick

Paperwork To Do Before School Begins

1. Make desk name tags for all of your students and have extras for students who enroll late. Use 5" x 8" (13 cm x 20 cm) blank file folder cards folded horizontally. For upper grades, write the students' names on one side and let them decorate the other. For primary grades, write their names on both sides because they get mixed up about which side goes towards you. They also need a handwriting sample to copy.

   Do not throw away the name tags you've made if students do not come—they may show up later in the week. Also, do not make a seating chart for the first couple of days because you may have students sitting next to each other who should not be, and it's much easier just to move the students and name tags than to change your writing on the seating chart.

2. Write lesson plans. Always plan for more than you think the students can do. The last thing you want is to run out of things and still have two hours left in your day. But if that does happen, go ahead and do the next day's work. It is better if they get upset at having math twice than if you have a panic attack. Besides, the first day they are more nervous than you are, and they aren't about to contradict you now. (That will come later in the year!)

3. Make a list of students on an assignment page. (See the Record Sheet for Assignments, page 96.) Copy this original list so you can also keep track of work and check off forms as they are returned. Make three copies and save the master. Your class will probably change in the first few days, so wait until later in the week to fill in the official register and lesson plan book, etc.

4. Establish discipline policies with students. (See pages 28–33.) Use the chart on page 112 as a guide.

S

Starting Off the Year *(cont.)*

Checklist for Getting Discipline Off to a Good Start

❑ Have your lessons clearly planned so students do not experience "down time."

❑ Keep parents informed about your class activities, discipline plan, homework, and how they can support your program.

❑ Set up simple, clear class rules and teach them to the students.

❑ Have both rewards and consequences for appropriate/inappropriate behavior established with your students.

❑ Communicate with parents early when a student is having problems at school.

❑ Follow school policy concerning suspensions, keeping students after school, and limiting recess or lunchtime.

❑ Be consistent, fair, and positive with students.

❑ Plan how to reward students for completing work assignments.

❑ Help students to feel successful, and they won't need to use disruptions or negative behavior for attention.

❑ Plan for what students are to do if they have trouble completing their work or if they finish early.

❑ Consider alternating between quiet, individual activities and more energetic group activities.

Starting Off the Year *(cont.)*

The Beginning Days

Handwriting: On the first or second day of school, have students practice their handwriting by copying from a textbook if you do not have a classroom library. Later in the week you can look over their handwriting and see what they need to work on. It's also nice to save their handwriting and return it to them the last week of school so they can see how much they have improved.

Math: At the beginning of the year, give students a test in math that covers a grade span from two below to one above the grade you are teaching to give you an idea of what the students need to review or learn. You might do a little review on the board first, taking up to three days, depending on your grade level, before giving the test, as students do forget skills over vacation.

Handling Books: In the first week, go over the parts of the book, including cover and spine, the table of contents, the glossary, and the index, as appropriate. Show the children how to turn pages and tell them that you expect them to treat all books with respect.

Standard Format: Tell students to write their names and the date on the upper right-hand corner of all papers. Explain that this will help you riffle through papers and find theirs easily, if need be. The title should go on the top line. Give them about a week to learn this; after that, if anyone's paper is incorrectly formatted, hand it back and ask the student to do it correctly.

Creative Writing: There are two projects which work well for the beginning of school for grades two through six. For the first idea, read aloud *The Teacher from the Black Lagoon*. Have them write "The Further Adventures" and illustrate the story.

The second idea is to write about their vacations—what didn't happen. (Perhaps it can be entitled, "My Summer—NOT!") They are to exaggerate everything and do a good job of describing what didn't happen. For those who might think that this is a form of lying, remember that students are merely telling what didn't happen. You can define what something is by what it is not.

Classroom Rules: On the first day, discuss and, if possible, display classroom rules with the students. (See page 28 for information on establishing classroom rules.) Send home a copy of your rules and expectations to parents and have students bring them back signed. Remind children that they come to school to learn and that no child should be an obstacle to this goal.

Starting Off the Year *(cont.)*

The Beginning Days *(cont.)*

School Rules: Students should all have a copy. Emphasize that the rules are for their safety. Walk the children around the school. Show them where the bathrooms are; remember that some of your students will be coming to school for the first time and may be too embarrassed to ask someone. Do not be afraid about not knowing the answer to everything. Instead of guessing, ask the long-time students for the answers.

Bulletin Boards: Before students arrive, put up boards that can be used year-round to display student work. Display captions for each subject and change only the student papers during the year. (Of course, there will be exceptions.)

Above the boards, add posters having to do with the subject, such as tips for creative writing, pictures related to social studies, etc. You may also be able to get book jackets from the library to pin up for the first week or so. An educational supply store should have pictures you can buy; think up a clever caption to tie them together. You do not want completely bare boards the first day. Ideas for year-round bulletin boards include the following:

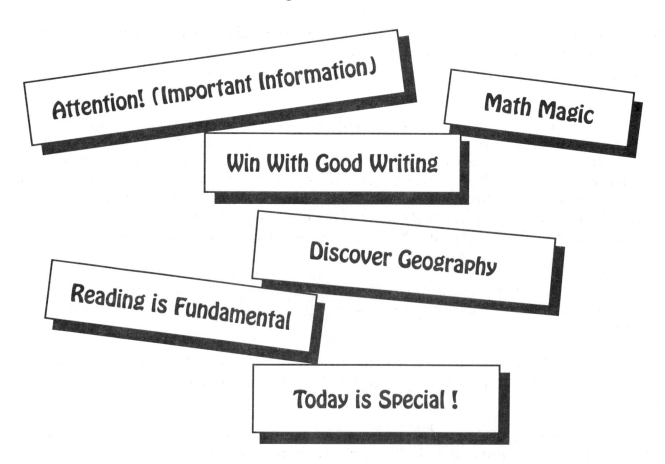

Also, post your name and the class list on the door with a welcoming sign. Post the rules, too.

Starting Off the Year (cont.)

The Beginning Days (cont.)

Desks: You will find a variety of seating charts on pages 98–103. There is a reason for this variety. Although students should be encouraged to interact with each other, every teacher has his or her own level of tolerance for talking in class. To encourage a quieter environment, especially during the first week or two, place the students in double rows; to encourage group work, place the students together in blocks. You may also determine that traditional seating is best for times when you have traditional lesson plans, and block seating is best for when you are using themes. Be flexible and find an arrangement that works best for both you and your students.

You may wish to allow students to choose the partners with whom they would like to sit. Make changes for those students who become disruptive when seated together. When students enter the room for the first time, have their name tags on their desks and their pencils, erasers, crayons, and textbooks ready for them. Students should write their names on their crayons and erasers with a small permanent marking pen; this can save a lot of hassle later. See also "Seating Charts," page 98, and "Group Work," p. 51.

Second Day Quiz: Consider giving the students a snap quiz on the second day of school on something they learned the first day. This will serve two purposes. First, they will learn to pay attention. Second, if you give the quizzes frequently, they will be less anxious about them and consequently do better on longer tests.

Student Absences: When students are absent during the year, it is their responsibility to make up any work they have missed. A study buddy should collect extra papers for them as they are passed out. (Ask the study buddy to put up a hand with two fingers raised to show he or she needs two papers as they are passed out.) Also keep a plastic hanging folder taped to a table with file folders inside labeled for the days of the week. When you copy things, make a few extra and put them in the appropriate folder. When a student returns, he or she needs to check with the study buddy to get the assignments, to look in the file folders for any work that has been missed, and to check in with you.

If it is unnecessary or impossible to make up the missed work, put a check in your grade book instead of a grade. But "I was absent when you assigned that" should not be an excuse unless the student has talked to you. Work that is not done or is incomplete counts as a fail after the first three missed assignments.

Students should also make up the work in a reasonable amount of time. If they are absent one day, they have one day to make it up; if absent two days, they have two days to make it up. After three days, they must speak to you.

Extended Absences: Children may take extended trips to visit their families—sometimes with very little warning. Because many school districts still receive money for a child if the teacher gives them work to do, it makes sense to keep a folder full of assignments handy. Then, when a child tells you, "I'm going away for three weeks!" you can just go to your file and pull out the forms and papers you need.

Starting Off the School Year *(cont.)*

The Beginning Days *(cont.)*

Extended Absences *(cont.)*: Do not put too much time into this, however, because you will probably find you have only about a 25% return rate. At the same time, you do want to make it worthwhile for motivated students.

Another handy thing to have is copies of chapters from old social studies and other texts. The student will be able to work at his or her own pace in these alternate texts, so that when the student returns he or she will not be out of step with the rest of the class.

For other ideas, or a form of which you can make several copies, see page 117.

Roll Call: If your school or district does not supply you with a roll call or grade book, prepare a roll call sheet for the beginning of the year. Use the form on page 118 or create one of your own. Write the students' names on the sheet before reproducing it. That way, you can reproduce as many copies as you need with the names already on the sheet.

Student Birthdays: To celebrate students' birthdays (if their special day is on a school day), let them choose the P.E. game for the day. This reward will be easy to remember; just write the birthdays in your lesson plan book at the beginning of the school year in the space reserved for P.E. The birthday children can choose to use rainy day or inside games if they wish, as well as the usual P.E. activities. You may also wish to present the child with a coupon, to be filled out the morning of the child's birthday (see below). In this way, both the student and the teacher will be prepared for the day's game. Sing "Happy Birthday" to them before playing the chosen game.

As an alternative, educational supply stores sell inexpensive pencils and stickers imprinted with "Happy Birthday" that children love to receive.

Happy Birthday!

This coupon entitles _____
(student's name)

to choose one activity/game today_____.
(date)

Choice

Have a great day!

Starting Off the School Year *(cont.)*
Activities for Extended Absences

Social Studies

1. Read all of the chapters I have attached.

2. Use complete sentences to answer all of the questions at the end of each section.

3. Study the countries in this unit and their bordering countries. Learn where they are and how to spell them. Also learn the major cities and geographic forms.

Math

Complete all of the work sheets I have attached.

Reading

Read a book and complete the following:

1. Write a summary of the book.

2. Find 20 new words, number them, and write synonyms or definitions for them. Remember that the words go on the edge of your paper. Use a margin for the definitions.

3. Choose two characters from the book and describe them—both their looks and qualities. Tell why you would or would not like to have one of them move next door to you.

Health

You have been contacted by the American Cancer Society. They would like you to write a magazine ad for a teen magazine, telling kids why they should not smoke. Write at least two paragraphs for the ad and submit a picture to go with it. (If you cannot draw it, you may get someone else to do that for you as long you give them credit. Or, you can do a rough sketch and label the things in your picture.)

Be sure that you have strong opening and closing sentences!

Grab the reader's attention!

Spelling

Make sure all work turned in is spelled correctly. It will count!

Have fun! We will miss you!

Starting Off the Year *(cont.)*

Roll Sheet

Name	Date																		

S

Student Dictionaries

This activity is especially good for lower grades or for students with undeveloped English or spelling skills. Make a sample student dictionary first, both to really see how to do it and to have an example for the students to follow when making their own. You and your students will be creating a composition notebook with a tab for each letter of the alphabet. This makes the dictionary easier to use, and the novelty of making tabs is an incentive.

Creating a Student Dictionary

Materials: composition notebook, marking pen, pencil, ruler, and scissors

1. Open up the composition notebook to the first page. Using your marking pen, write a capital letter A on the far right side of the first line and then turn the page and write a capital letter B on the second line. Continue turning pages and writing a letter of the alphabet until you reach either the end of the alphabet or the end of the lines. If you reach the end of the lines first, turn the page and put the next letter of the alphabet on the top of the next line.

2. Create a letter tab for A by drawing a vertical line from the horizontal line the A sits on to the bottom of the page. Turn to the page with the letter B and draw a vertical line from the horizontal line the letter sits on. Repeat this process until the book is complete.

3. Use scissors to cut the vertical line on each page. Then cut the horizontal line under the letter on that page. (See illustration.)

4 You now have a book with tabs so you can easily find the letter of the alphabet under which you will want to write new words.

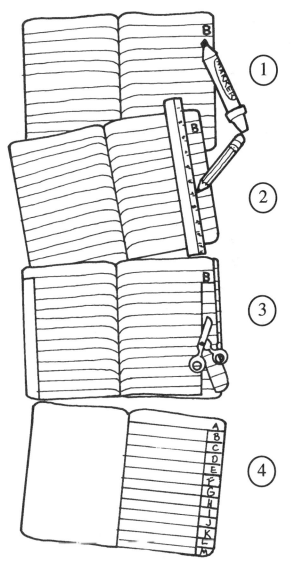

Also, any time you need to ask someone to spell a word, bring along your student dictionary—open to the correct page—and a pencil.

Students as Teachers

In the upper grades, it's a good learning experience for both you and the class to have a day when the students can become teachers. If you decide to do this, list all the possible subjects students might wish to teach on the chalkboard; allow them to help you with this. Then ask them to fill out an application form (page 121) and let them work with a partner if they wish. Tell them you will choose only the best application for each subject. Also, the students are not required to do the work for that subject, but they are to grade the papers—if any—as part of their grade. If a speech is also assigned for that week (see pages 104–105), their teaching work may count in its place.

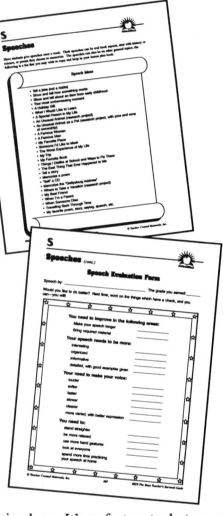

Study Buddies

Ask students to pair up with study buddies in your classroom. That way, they have someone to ask what has been assigned or how to do something. If they are absent, the study buddy can bring work to them or just write down the assignments as they are given. They should try to find someone who lives close by. You may also want to get signed parent permission slips allowing children to exchange phone numbers. Please emphasize to the students that phone numbers are private and are not to be passed out to others.

Subject Reviews

When it comes time for tests, give your students a chance to study in class. It's unfortunate, but many students do not have a quiet place at home to study. It doesn't do any harm, and it may do some good, to allow them time to study.

Students can study with partners for map tests, math facts, etc., but try putting them into teams for science and social studies. They get a period (or two) to write questions from their textbooks on 3"x 5" (8 cm x 13 cm) cards. Number the cards and number the answers and the page in the text on which it can be found on a corresponding answer sheet. Students can prepare (study) that night for the next day's contest patterned after a popular TV quiz show where each group can come up with answers to earn points.

It makes it more interesting if each group gets to write a 20-point question for the end of the contest and groups get to wager the points they have earned so far. If a group's questions are rotated, then when they make up the questions they stay pretty quiet so another group can't hear the questions they are writing and look up the answers ahead of time.

Student's Teaching Application

Name or names of teachers: _____

Subject you'd like to teach: _____

What you will teach for that subject (page, name of skill, etc.)? _____

What you expect students to learn: _____

_____

How will you evaluate the learning that takes place? Will you grade papers, take notes on students who participate, etc.?

_____

_____

_____

List any material you will need on the back of this page. Put a star next to the items you want your teacher to provide.

Student's Teaching Application

Name or names of teachers: _____

Subject you'd like to teach: _____

What you will teach for that subject (page, name of skill, etc.)? _____

What you expect students to learn: _____

_____

How will you evaluate the learning that takes place? Will you grade papers, take notes on students who participate, etc.?

_____

_____

_____

List any material you will need on the back of this page. Put a star next to the items you want your teacher to provide.

S

Substitutes

Getting Ready for a Substitute

As soon as you can, get together a box of items that you can leave for a substitute in case of an emergency. Ask an experienced teacher for help or get some duplicating masters from the teacher supply store. The box should include work and art ideas that can be done at anytime during the year, such as work in alphabetical order, puzzles for math, reading comprehension work sheets, etc.

Getting ready for a substitute when you know you will need one (and doing a good job) can take about an hour to an hour and a half or more. It helps if you have this information in the front of your lesson plan book or some other readily available place so that you do not need to write plans for the substitute each time. Also, your lesson plans, methods, and disciplinary procedures will also be more completely explained.

Not only do you need a plan, you also need to have a box that substitutes can go to for materials that are already run off if they are not prepared, do not understand your plans, have extra time, or the copy machine is broken.

If You Are a Substitute

As soon as you are hired, have materials ready for all the grades you will teach. The best investment may be a few books that cover grade levels by skill rather than by subject. However, you should not use them unless there is an emergency (for example, the teacher has not left any lesson plans or you do not understand how to do something). Have work sheets copied ahead of time in case the copying machine is broken or you are called late to an assignment. In fact, keep folders of grade level work at home so that when you do get called half an hour before school starts, you can just grab the folder and run. Remember, too, that you can use the chalkboard or overhead projector for many assignments.

Should the copy machine be broken and you become desperate, ask a fellow teacher for help. Many teachers have extra stacks of work sheets somewhere that they planned on using but found they didn't need or have time to use.

You may also have some easy, handy ideas that can be used by children at many grade levels. There are some good math games you can do without any preparations (but it's much easier if you have paper handy).

Ideas for Substitutes

Indoor Games: Play "Bang" to review multiplication facts or "Silent Ball" if you have a ball. (See "Indoor Games," page 46.)

Letter Jumble: For this project, there are usually upcoming holidays that you can use to do this time filler. Have students use the letters of the holiday to make as many words as possible. Use of dictionaries should be encouraged. Students are to use only the letters that are found in the word and if there is only one a, then their new word may have only one a in it. Children must be able to tell you what a word means, so if they think you might not know it, they are to write the meaning down to prove that it's really a word. Offer a small reward; carry inexpensive stickers with you for this purpose.

You might want to make—or have the children make—strips of paper with the word written on them—in block letters if you're in primary class. They can then cut the letters apart and move them around.

If there is no upcoming holiday, then use a good, long word or short phrase from science or social studies, their reading book, etc. Allowing them to work in partners usually goes well if you remind them that they need to be quiet so another team doesn't overhear them.

Math Shape Art: Draw different geometric shapes on the chalkboard. Talk about the attributes of squares, circles, triangles (both isosceles and equilateral if you need them), rectangles, ovals, etc. Assign each group or row to a different shape and tell them they may use only that shape on their drawing paper. Shapes may be overlapping, of different sizes, and rotated. After they have filled their paper with shapes (using rulers for straight edges and black marking pens to make the outlines if they are available), they are to take their crayons and, pressing very hard, fill in each area. No color should touch another like-colored area. These projects look nice when they are done and take about an hour.

The One Dollar Word Game: Letters in the alphabet are given increasing money values in sequential order: a=$.01, b=$.02, c=$.03, etc. Make a list of the value of the letters on the chalkboard and then find the "worth" of simple things like "desk," and "chair," and "pencil." Children then try to figure out the value of their own names, and finally they can try to find any words that equal a dollar. (You might want to prove to them that it can be done with the word "elephant.")

Alphabetizing: Alphabetizing is usually a good project for students. Alphabetizing activities are provided on pages 125 and 126. If you do not have time to copy these pages, write them on the board—it will take longer anyway

Sponge Activities: These are brief activities that productively engage the students. They may be given to students during transition periods, as students and teachers begin the morning's activities, or as a way of refocusing students on something they have previously learned. Sponge activities are ideal for substitutes to use with the whole class, small groups, or individuals at strategic times of the day. (See pages 127 and 128 for sponge activities.)

S

Substitutes

Substitute's Log

Dear Substitute,

Please list the lesson plans and activities you implemented today. In the space provided, be sure to describe, in the space provided, any problems you experienced during your day here. Thank you for helping me out today.

Your name: _____ Today's date: _____

Subject: _____	Subject: _____	Subject: _____
Comments:	Comments:	Comments:
Subject: _____	Subject: _____	Subject: _____
Comments:	Comments:	Comments:

Substitutes *(cont.)*

Alphabetical Order

Put the following pairs of words in alphabetical order.

1. bear, zebra

_____

_____

2. cat, monkey

_____

_____

3. pants, brush

_____

_____

4. hair, foot

_____

_____

5. school, desk

_____

_____

6. chalk, paper

_____

_____

7. radio, television

_____

_____

8. rat, hamster

_____

_____

9. book, notebook

_____

_____

10. kitchen, den

_____

_____

11. pillow, lamp

_____

_____

12. hen, rooster

_____

_____

13. sheep, cow

_____

_____

14. cat, truck

_____

_____

15. sand, beach

_____

_____

16. newspaper, morning

_____

_____

17. doll, drum

_____

_____

18. rabbit, run

_____

_____

19. frosty, fox

_____

_____

20. blanket, bed

_____

_____

21. land, log

_____

_____

22. horse, heat

_____

_____

23. fan, furniture

_____

_____

24. dog, doghouse

_____

_____

Substitutes *(cont.)*

Alphabetical Order

Put the following groups of words in alphabetical order.

A. flux, guidebook, halogen, cytology, ideal, pair, wolverine, flurry, dross, growl, festive, paddock, north, doubtless, identify, gambol, drowse, guise

1. _____
2. _____
3. _____
4. _____
5. _____
6. _____
7. _____
8. _____
9. _____
10. _____
11. _____
12. _____
13. _____
14. _____
15. _____
16. _____
17. _____
18. _____

B. feeling, fear, finger, fight, fall, feed, fast, feel, field, foster, finite, favor, fortify, failure, feedback, finding, fashion, faint

1. _____
2. _____
3. _____
4. _____
5. _____
6. _____
7. _____
8. _____
9. _____
10. _____
11. _____
12. _____
13. _____
14. _____
15. _____
16. _____
17. _____
18. _____

C. heal, hear, headlock, heath, heavy, heart, heat, head, headway, hearth, heathen, heater, headline, headphone, healthful, heartache, heap, health

1. _____
2. _____
3. _____
4. _____
5. _____
6. _____
7. _____
8. _____
9. _____
10. _____
11. _____
12. _____
13. _____
14. _____
15. _____
16. _____
17. _____
18. _____

S

Super Sponge Activities

1. Play 5 X 5. This is easily accomplished by making a grid of 25 squares. Choose five categories. Place one on the top of each box. Then randomly choose five letters and place one on each box down the side. Have students call out words that fit each category. This is really handy when working with a theme that you wish to review.

2. The game of Charades is a an enjoyable sponge activity, especially when used as a review. Use spelling or vocabulary words, titles of books by authors the class has studied, or activities going on in school. Put these on slips of paper and place in a container. Let individuals or groups of students choose one and act it out.

3. Read aloud to your class! Keep some funny, short stories or a book of limericks available for a quick read.

4. Play "baseball." Choose a skill that needs to be reviewed. Draw a baseball diamond on the board. Choose a scorekeeper. Divide the class into two teams. Determine which team is up first. Ask each player a review question. If the player answers correctly, have him or her run the bases by marking the base on the diamond on the board. A run is scored every time a player touches home base. If the team misses three questions, the other team is up.

5. Try some rhythms. Clap or tap out a rhythm and then have students repeat it. Vary the patterns and the lengths, making them increasingly more challenging.

6. Choose a category such as food, movies, or places, and challenge students to think of one for each letter of the alphabet.

7. Select a category, such as famous people. Have one student say the name. The next student must name another famous person whose first name begins with the last letter of the person's name.

8. Ask students a number of questions, such as these: "Is there anyone whose digits in his/her phone number add up to 30?" "Whose birthday is closest to the date when man first walked on the moon (or any other date you have been studying)?" "If you add the ages of everyone in your family, who has the highest number? Who has the lowest?"

9. Create a spelling chain. All students stand. Give them a spelling word. The first person says the first letter, the second gives the second letter, and so on. If a student gives the wrong letter, he/she must sit down.

10. Play "Guess the Characteristic." Ask several students that have something in common to stand. The class, including the standing students, must guess what they all have in common, such as they all have shoes with no laces, they all walk to school, or they all are in band.

11. Do a daily edit to start the day or fill small spaces of time. These become writing skill mini-lessons. Lift an incorrect sentence directly from student writing or create one that includes errors that students are commonly making. You may wish to focus on one skill at a time. Print the incorrect sentence(s) on the board or overhead. Have students edit the sentence and write it correctly into a section of their journal or a special notebook that can be used for reference. Follow up at some time during the day with a class discussion so the students may finalize their corrections and see that there may be more than one way to solve a writing problem.

12. An especially effective daily edit that promotes more interesting writing is "Expand a Sentence." Give students a very simple sentence, such as The ∧child ran∧. Include insert marks where you want students to add words and underline words that they may change to something more exciting. Model an expansion for students the first time you do this activity. The new sentence may become "The very excited young lady raced wildly down the street with her red braids flying straight out behind her."

13. Keep a supply of board and table games that require strategy and thinking. Use them for special fill-in times like rainy day recesses. Good examples are Scrabble, Monopoly, Boggle, and Chutes and Ladders.

14. Collect word searches, crossword puzzles, kid's pages from Sunday comics, and Mad Libs. Laminate them for wipe-off reuse.

15. Save about-to-be discarded paper with at least one blank side, computer printouts, old dittos, faded construction paper, etc. Use for free-drawing time. Also encourage students to free-write; many of them also improve creativity and expertise in drawing with practice.

16. Derive many words from one. Copy on the blackboard a multisyllabic word taken from a theme or topic of the day. Ask students to write as many words from this as they can in a specified time. Only letters from the original word may be used. This activity can be done in small groups or individually.

17. Set up a magnetic board center for sponge activities. Divide the board into yes and no columns. Prepare a magnetic name tag for each student by gluing a tagboard square with the student's name onto a piece of magnetic strip (available at fabric or sign stores). On the board, pose daily questions which involve critical thinking, opinions, or problem solving activities. The questions must have yes or no answers. Have students place their magnetic name tags in the appropriate column. Discuss responses.

18. Read a short story, poem, essay, news article, etc., to the class. Have students write a short first impression of it. Compare student responses.

19. Play "Three-in-a-Row." Make game boards from 8 ½" x 11" (21 cm x 28 cm) pieces of tagboard, cardboard, or index paper. Divide each game board into nine equal boxes. Provide X and O cards (five of each) for each game board (be sure cards fit into the boxes).

    Two students use one game board, one using X cards and the other using O cards. Use this game for reinforcement or review. When a student responds correctly to a problem or activity, he/she places a card in a box. If the response is incorrect, the player loses a turn. The first player to achieve three in a row vertically, horizontally, or diagonally is the winner.

20. Incorporate a "Brain Teaser Time" into your day. Choose from a selection of brain teaser activities or have students make up some of their own. These can be presented to the class as part of your daily sponge activities.

Weekly Goals

When setting goals, it is important to put them in writing and to determine the steps and materials necessary to achieve them. You can set daily, weekly, or long-term goals. The following form is provided in this section to assist you with your goal-setting.

	Goals	Materials	Comments
Monday			
Tuesday			
Wednesday			
Thursday			
Friday			

Weekly Reports

Weekly reports on each student do take time—at least two hours per week at the beginning—but in the long run it will be well worth the effort. Parents generally welcome this information, and children who are performing well will get a boost in confidence. Another advantage is that parents of children who are not performing well will not become irate when you share negative information with them on parent conference day.

Keep the current reports handy on your desk so that you can immediately record any misbehavior or good deed. Also be sure to fill in any incomplete assignments and add any comments you wish to make. In order to make this job simpler, keep an extra copy of a weekly report in the folder and copy down the assignments from the chalkboard every day after school. Then you will have the assignments and due dates handy and can easily write missed work on the students' reports. Also mark each student's absences and tardies on the weekly report. Be aware that sometimes these are a surprise to the parents!

Tuesday is a traditional day to send bulletins home in many districts, and this may be a good day for you to send home the weekly reports. Allow students time to read what you have written about the work in their folders. This feedback is a benefit to the student. The week's work then goes home with the Weekly Report which is to be signed by their parents. Collect the signed Weekly Reports during roll call on Wednesday. If students return signed reports on time, give them a raffle ticket. If the reports are not back by Thursday, call the parents and let them know what has happened. Remind parents that the reports go home weekly and need to be signed.

Encourage parents to write down any questions or comments they may have on the back of the reports. You may also staple important letters to parents to the Weekly Report. You will have better communication with your parents because of it.

For those students who do not get back on track with weekly reports, use a daily contract (see pages 134-135) to go with it. During a parent conference, explain that as soon as the contract comes back signed by all concerned parties, you will begin sending home a daily report. The daily report brings about improvement in most students. If it doesn't, let the parents know that the daily report is not effective for their child and that you are concerned about the student's lack of progress. At this point, it might be a good idea to bring in someone from the administration for support or make a referral to the school psychologist. Quite often what seems to be disruptive behavior is a sign of a learning disability. Research shows that 10–30% of the population has a learning disability of some type, so consider whether the behavior you are observing is a call for help. Either way, further assessment may be needed to determine if the student has special needs of one sort or another that cannot be remedied without additional resources.

For those students for whom weekly reports are enough, there are copies of reports in English and Spanish (pages 131 and 132). Reproduce them in different colors so it's easier for the students to identify their language when they pick them up. If you wish to include subjects or activities other than the ones listed on page 131, use the blank form on page 133.

In addition to weekly and daily report forms, a student assignment sheet and a home reading record form are provided on pages 136 and 137.

Weekly Reports *(cont.)*

Weekly Report

(English)

Name _____   Date _____

Subject	Monday	Tuesday	Wednesday	Thursday	Friday
Reading					
Home Reading					
Language					
Oral Language					
Writing					
Math					
Science/Health					
Social Studies					
Notes/Forms not returned					
Behavior					

☐ Completed work not turned in on time   ☐ Unsatisfactory

_____
Parent's Signature

Weekly Reports *(cont.)*

Weekly Report
(Spanish)

Name_____   Date _____

	Lunes	Martes	Miercoles	Jueves	Viernes
Lectura					
Lectura en casa					
Artes de Lenguaje					
Comunicación oral					
Escritura					
Matemáticas					
Ciencias					
Estudios Sociales					
Notas/Formas: No regresadas					
Comportamiento					

☐ Trabajo terminado que no ha entregado   ☐ No-satisfactorio

_____
Firma de los padres

Weekly Reports *(cont.)*

Weekly Report

(Blank Form)

Name _____   Date _____

Subject/Activity	Monday	Tuesday	Wednesday	Thursday	Friday

☐   Completed work not
turned in on time

☐   Unsatisfactory

_____
Parent's Signature

Weekly Reports *(cont.)*

Contract for Daily Reports

(English)

Dear Parents and Student,

Please make up a contract together by completing the following steps:

1. Decide what small reward (stay up 15 minutes late, earn an extra bedtime story, be allowed to talk on the phone, for example) will be given if all the assigned work is done. This reward should be given each day that the student brings home a good Daily Report and fulfills the contract.

2. Decide what disciplinary action (early bedtime, no phone privileges, for example) will occur when the student does not fulfill the contract.

3. Write down the reward and punishment you have all agreed upon.

4. All parties need to sign the contract.

5. Return the contract to school so that the teacher can sign the contract, make a copy, and return the original to you. The contract should be posted in a prominent place so it can be referred to when necessary.

Daily reward:_____

Disciplinary action: _____

Student's signature: _____

Parent's or Guardian's signature:_____

Teacher's signature: _____

Reminder: The students must . . .

> . . . bring the weekly report home everyday.
> . . . have no marks in any space.
> . . . have daily assignments copied from the board and take the assignments home every day, or he or she is to be punished. If there are any marks in any space, the student is to be punished.

Accept **no** excuses for a report or work left at school.

Thank you. Together we can make this a productive, interesting, and rewarding school year.

Weekly Reports *(cont.)*

Contract for Daily Reports
(Spanish)

Estimados padres y estudiante,

Por favor hagan un contrato. Juntos necesitan:

1. Decidir que cosa buena (pequena) sucedera si todo el trabao asignado se termina. Este premio se dara todos los dias que el estudiante traiga a casa un buen contrato.

2. Decidir que cosa (pequena, pero importante) sucedera todos los dias que el estudiante no termine el contrato.

3. Poner por escrito el premio y castigo que todos han concordado dar.

4. Todos los grupos necesitan firmer el contrato.

5. Devolver el contrato a la escuela para que la maestro. Martin pueda firmer el contrato, hacer una copia, y devolverles el original a ustedes para que el contrato pueda colocarce en un lugar prominete y se pueda referir a ello cuando sea necesario.

Premio diario: _____

Castigo diario:_____

Firma del estudiante: _____

Firma de padre o madre: _____

Firma de la maestra: _____

Redordatorio: El estudiante debe . . .

     . . . tener la forma diario.

     . . . no tener marcas en algun espacio.

     . . . tener asisgnaciones diaries copiadas atras, o el/ella sera castigado/s.

Si todos los expacios son vacios, el/ella sera permidado/a. **NO** se aceptan escusas por espacios con marcos o por un contrato dejado en la escuela.

Gracias! Juntos podemos hacer que este ano escolar sea productivo, interesante, y remunerador!

Weekly Reports *(cont.)*
Student Assignments

Copy the assignments from the board and then take this to the teacher to get initialed.

Monday   1. _____

┌─────────────┐   2. _____
│ Teacher's │   3. _____
│   Initials │   4. _____
│   │   5. _____
└─────────────┘

Tuesday   1. _____

┌─────────────┐   2. _____
│ Teacher's │   3. _____
│   Initials │   4. _____
│   │   5. _____
└─────────────┘

Wednesday   1. _____

┌─────────────┐   2. _____
│ Teacher's │   3. _____
│   Initials │   4. _____
│   │   5. _____
└─────────────┘

Thursday   1. _____

┌─────────────┐   2. _____
│ Teacher's │   3. _____
│   Initials │   4. _____
│   │   5. _____
└─────────────┘

Friday   1. _____

┌─────────────┐   2. _____
│ Teacher's │   3. _____
│   Initials │   4. _____
│   │   5. _____
└─────────────┘

Weekly Reports

Weekly Home Reading Records

Dates: _____ to _____

Day	Time	Read To
Sunday		
Monday		
Tuesday		
Wednesday		
Thursday		
Friday		
Saturday		

Student _____ Parent _____

Student _____ Teacher _____

Day & Date	What Was Read
Monday	
Tuesday	
Wednesday	
Thursday	
Friday	
Saturday	
Sunday	

Parent's Signature _____

X-tra Ideas—The Terrific 20s

20 Ways to Prevent Burnout

1. When you feel overwhelmed by the demands of school, use some of the excellent videos, films, and TV programs that will enrich your lesson plans and give you a momentary break.

2. Make use of seasonal activity sheets to jazz up routine lessons. Keep them as simple as math facts written inside of hearts for Valentine's Day or pumpkins for Halloween.

3. Go to workshops. Perhaps your district will pay. But, even if you have to pay for them yourself, they are worth the money in terms of the new outlook and enthusiasm they engender.

4. Take some classes that get you credit on your district's salary schedule.

5. Take some classes just for fun. Try some areas that have little or nothing to do with education or children. Exposure to almost anything will eventually pay off in the classroom, and you will have fun and meet new people.

6. Attend art gallery showings and bookstore signings. You will see that there are adults in the real world and get rid of that "trapped" feeling one gets from being too long in a classroom with thirty young children. Besides, they are free.

7. Incorporate more art in your lesson plans. It can be a real enrichment to your literature and social studies units and, besides, it gives everyone's spirits a lift.

8. Learn a lot of new classroom games and play them. Don't save them for special times. Intersperse them throughout the day.

9. Have parties from time to time for no special reason other than to have fun.

10. Try acting the way you would like to be feeling. There is a school of psychological thought that holds that we begin to feel the way we act. Go around smiling and looking happy and enthusiastic and see if you start to feel that way. It is certainly worth a try.

11. Jump-start your helper system if it has started to fall apart on you. There are times of the year when parents get busy at home and begin to send regrets instead of coming in to help. Send home a note asking for assistance.

12. Spend some time re-bonding with your class. Things sometimes start to go sour halfway through the year.

13. Take a vacation. The next time there is a three-day weekend, go somewhere.

14. Consider having someone come in and clean your house or complete a longstanding household project. Even if it is just for one time, it will give you a wonderful new start.

15. Sit at a different table for lunch in your teachers' room. Talk to someone new.

16. Take on a volunteer position for some charity that appeals to you. Doing something for other people often lifts one's spirits tremendously.

17. Get a part-time job. Sometimes the change of pace (and the extra cash) is just what you need to prevent burnout.

18. Work through your lunch break and meet a friend after school for a late lunch at a restaurant.

19. Stop saying you are "going to school." Say you are "going to work." It's a real job.

20. Read and implement everything you can find about self-esteem techniques.

X-tra Ideas—The Terrific 20s *(cont.)*

20 Money-Saving Ideas

1. Use the plastic "popcorn" from packages for art projects and math counters.

2. Ask at your local newspaper for leftover newsprint for art projects and drawing paper.

3. Scout out companies that use computer paper. They often discard the last few inches of a stack of paper rather than risk running out while printing.

4. Swap and share with other teachers rather than buying duplicate supplies.

5. Check magazines and newspapers for coupons and free offers.

6. Invest in fade-proof paper to back your bulletin boards. It will last all year.

7. Save all kinds of containers—margarine tubs, coffee cans, oatmeal cartons, and so on—for storing games and math manipulatives.

8. Send home a monthly class newsletter and ask parents to save things for art and science projects.

9. Buy or borrow a book such as *500 Free Things for Kids to Do and Send For.*

10. Use macaroni or other pastas in different shapes for counters, art projects, and so on.

11. Ask stores for used seasonal advertising displays—hearts, bunnies, Santas, and so on. Cut off or cover up the advertising and use them for dramatic bulletin board accents.

12. If your district has a media lab, use it to create games, charts, and activities.

13. Ask students to bring a favorite (or extra) game from home to use in the classroom on rainy days.

14. Ask parents and students to go through their books. If they are no longer using them, they may want to donate them to your classroom library.

15. Look for children's books at garage sales and swap meets and add them to your classroom library.

16. Stir up some salt and flour modeling dough. You can keep it for quite awhile in airtight containers for reuse, or you can bake the results of the students' projects for use as permanent ornaments, paperweights, etc.

17. If you buy treats for your class, purchase them in large quantities at a discount store.

18. Look through the advertising materials you get through the mail at work. They often contain posters, maps, or stickers.

19. Keep leftover activity sheets. Use the backs for scratch paper.

20. Remember that time and money are interchangeable. Spend time to save money.

X-tra Ideas—The Terrific 20s *(cont.)*

20 Time-Saving Ideas

1. Let the students take turns doing your filing. They will learn ABC order, and you can do something else. Teach one or two students and let them each teach another and so on.

2. Walk around the room and correct work during the lesson rather doing it after school.

3. Don't prepare so much ahead of time—let the students do their own tracing and cutting.

4. Buy punch-out letters for your bulletin board captions.

5. If you have an aide or reliable parent helpers, decide what you want to do yourself and then delegate the other tasks.

6. Have students grade their own or each other's papers. If you are using the writing process, peer editing fits in here.

7. Use your student room helpers efficiently. You won't ever have to put another paper in a mailbox or water another plant.

8. Keep some personal things tucked away in your room. A soft drink and a box of crackers will get you through a lunch hour and save you from having to stay after school on a day when you must get to an important meeting or appointment.

9. Get in the habit of making double plans. If you have an art lesson every Friday, make next Friday's plan and then, while you are thinking about it, flip ahead in your plan book and do another plan for another lesson.

10. The next time you have a staff meeting, carry along papers to grade or something to cut out while you are waiting for the meeting to begin or when there are pauses or interruptions in the proceedings.

11. Volunteer carefully. If you are going to agree to do something that will take a lot of time, make sure it is something you really enjoy and that you can really spare the time.

12. Ask parent helpers to do things like running off sets of papers, stapling, and laminating.

13. Spend an occasional weekend day in your classroom and get completely organized for a month ahead to save time on a daily basis.

14. Pay someone to grade papers for you on an occasional or regular basis. A volunteer or assistant at your school may appreciate extra take-home work. High school students are sometimes available for this kind of work.

15. Give a daily review, including the various skills that should be reinforced for end-of-year testing. You will avoid spending a lot of time on last minute catch-up.

16. Spend the first six weeks of the year concentrating on bonding and team building with your students. You will save the time that you would otherwise spend on discipline and classroom management later in the year.

17. Use the services that are offered by library resource people. They will do research and get you information that you need.

18. If you keep your teaching project centered and do a thorough task analysis, completion of the project will show mastery of the skills embedded in the project without need for further assessment.

19. Get older students, from another classroom if necessary, to help you with everyday room cleanup.

20. Remember that time and money are interchangeable. Spend money to save time.

X-tra Ideas—The Terrific 20s *(cont.)*

20 Terrific Bulletin Board Ideas

1. Create a bulletin board using real books or book jackets. Display the books on a bulletin board that the class is currently reading. These can form a path that is entitled "The Road to Learning."

2. Cover your bulletin board with newspaper. Cut or punch out letters that read Good News! Then display students' best efforts.

3. Have a "We Have Visited_____" bulletin board. Encourage students to bring in brochures, post-cards, and photos from places they have traveled.

4. A classroom management bulletin board can stay up all year and help keep you organized. Include your helper chart, class calendar, school bulletins, copies of assignments, and other important information. This becomes a teaching tool as you do calendar activities with students and change the helper chart.

5. Use brown butcher paper and make a tree. Scrunch the paper up into the shape of the trunk and branches of a tree. Staple it against a background of green for the grass and blue for the sky. Add leaves to it for each season. Use the leaves to display math problems, theme words, or anything that your class would want to share.

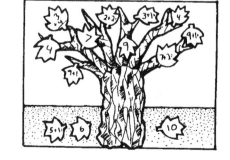

6. Maps make great backgrounds for bulletin boards. Big maps that can be written or drawn on can be used to cover large areas. Student work relating to the map can then be hung on the map. Maps can also be the focal point of the bulletin board, with questions such as "Where in the World Were You Born?" as a label and pushpins available for children to mark the locations of the answers. Children also love being able to follow a character's adventure in a book or pinpointing where their grandparents live.

X-tra Ideas—The Terrific 20s *(cont.)*

20 Terrific Bulletin Board Ideas *(cont.)*

7. Let students have a brag board. Divide a bulletin board into enough squares for each student. Explain to them that this is their own space to display anything they want, such as pictures of family members, work they are proud of, awards, recipes they wish to share, free pet announcements, etc. Tell students they are responsible for changing the materials.

8. Make a bulletin board of a computer keyboard by using foam hamburger containers with letters or numbers written on them to represent the keys. Put three together for the space bar and two for the shift keys. Title it "We're All Keyed Up."

9. Make a large gumball machine. Add a construction paper gumball each day the class meets a predetermined goal, such as perfect attendance, everyone completed homework, good behavior, etc. When the gumball machine is full, reward the class.

10. Pose a challenging "Whoo Knows?" question of the day in the center of the bulletin board, written in a nest or hole in a tree. Any students who correctly answer the question may write their names on a precut owl and hang it on the board.

11. Have a "Reading Is a Blast" bulletin board. In the center of the board, have a picture of a rocket. After students have completed books, they may write their names and the titles of the books on precut planets, stars, or astronauts and attach them to the board.

12. Let students help create a mural bulletin board relating to a topic being studied. You provide a simple background and students add cutouts that they have drawn and colored. For example, when studying kinds of transportation, you provide a dark blue river or lake, brown land, and light-blue sky. Students add appropriate vehicles to each area.

X-tra Ideas—The Terrific 20s *(cont.)*

20 Terrific Bulletin Board Ideas *(cont.)*

13. To jazz up your bulletin boards, add real objects, such as string for kites, bottle caps for wheels, thick yarn for stems, egg carton cups for petals, Easter grass, dried autumn leaves, balloons, cotton batting for snow, sandpaper for sand, and so forth. Glue or staples will secure most of these items.

14. Make changing bulletin boards easy by planning ahead. The purchase of nonfade bulletin board paper in a color that matches your room provides a permanent bright background for those bulletin boards that will stay up all year. Use contact paper, wrapping paper, or wallpaper for patterned backgrounds. Colored corrugated paper available in teacher supply stores provide an attractive textured background to which it is easy to pin student work or displays. If you have access to a press-punch machine that cuts letters, follow this procedure to make letter sets from which you can quickly pull your bulletin board titles all year. Laminate several sheets of several colors of construction paper. Cut the sheets into strips the proper width for the letter machine. Stack as many sheets, one of each color, as your machine will cut at one time. Cut several of each vowel and the common consonants and one or two for the less common. Save some extra laminated strips of each color to trace letters that you may run out of. Store the sets by color in large envelopes. When putting up a new bulletin board, you simply choose the letters you need.

15. Make a simple sign-up spot for center activities on a bulletin board. Write center names or draw an identifying picture and the number of students allowed at each center on 2" x 8" (5 cm x 20 cm) strips of tagboard. Staple these strips onto a bulletin board, allowing them to bow out from the background. Store wooden clip clothespins on which students' names have been written in a container near the bulletin board. Students sign up for a center by clipping their clothespins to a strip. When the number of clothespins on a strip matches the number written on the strip, the center is closed to additional sign-ups. An alternative is to use library card pockets and paper name strips for sign-ups.

X-tra Ideas—The Terrific 20s *(cont.)*

20 Terrific Bulletin Board Ideas *(cont.)*

16. When you find a magazine or newspaper picture spread that is appropriate for a subject you are studying, display it to share it most effectively. Mount pictures on construction paper, write captions or titles on contrasting construction paper strips, and arrange all on a colorful background. **Hint**: Buy two copies so you can display both sides. Be sure to store the pictures and captions for use another year.

17. Pique student curiosity and anticipation in your classroom with a "Coming Soon" bulletin board. In the center, prepare a marquis in a frame that features the new topic or event and presents interesting information about the upcoming unit. Surround the frame with relevant objects, pictures, etc. Place a manila envelope in a corner of the bulletin board or leave a shoe box near it for students to deposit cards containing questions that they may wish to ask or learn about the topic. When you are ready to begin the unit, your students will be prepared and eager as well.

18. A bulletin board featuring a Thought for the Week can promote positive classroom discussions, writing activities, and related projects. Use titles such as "Words of Wisdom", "Think About It," or "In My Opinion." This type of bulletin board should be simple and thought provoking. Well-known phrases such as "A penny saved is a penny earned," or "The early bird catches the worm," lend themselves to discussion and activities on good habits. Use it as a year-round interactive bulletin board and surround it with students' ideas, interpretations, and suggestions relating to the topic.

19. Students enjoy seeing their photos displayed in the classroom. Take pictures of each student. Prepare a bulletin board in which student photos may be used for a variety of purposes, such as classroom job assignments, to accompany writing activities or opinion polls, and to feature a student of the week or students involved in a cooperative group presentation. For young children, make a large calendar bulletin board and place a student's photo in each weekday box. The day in which the student is featured becomes his/her "special day."

20. Make a match-up bulletin board in which students can match information, pictures, or ideas from one column with those in another. Glue acetate sheets to cardboard, tagboard, or index paper which has been cut to form frames. The acetate creates a window through which match-up cards can be seen. Staple the window frames into two equal columns (be sure to leave the top of the frame open for depositing match-up cards). This bulletin board can be used throughout the year.